It is often assumed that children are the main victims of divorce. Very often that is true, but if your separation is handled with care you can make sure your children suffer as little as possible. Anne Hooper takes the reader through a section of the common questions that children ask such as 'Mummy, why doesn't Daddy like you any more?' She also discusses such questions as the relationship between step-parents and step-children; how to explain a new sex life to children; the law on custody and access – both in terms of legal rights and real life practice; and the emotional problems your children are most likely to encounter. She has interviewed many divorced couples, and also some of their children, to find how they coped with the difficulties they encountered and combines their experiences with a great deal of practical information, including details of agencies that offer divorce counselling and other forms of help.

Anne Hooper is a marriage and divorce counsellor and frequently gives advice about emotional problems on the radio. She decided to write *Divorce and Your Children* following her own separation, when she and her ex-husband found it very difficult to obtain specific practical help on wha̲̍ ̲̍ ̲̍ ̲̍ ̲̍ ̲̍ ̲̍ ̲̍ ̲̍ ̲̍ ̲̍ children.

Divorce and Your Children

ANNE HOOPER

London
UNWIN PAPERBACKS
Boston   Sydney

First published in Great Britain by George Allen & Unwin 1981
First published by Unwin Paperbacks 1983

UNWIN® PAPERBACKS
40 Museum Street, London WC1A 1LU, UK

Unwin Paperbacks,
Park Lane, Hemel Hempstead, Herts HP2 4TE, UK

George Allen & Unwin Australia Pty Ltd,
8 Napier Street, North Sydney, NSW 2060, Australia

British Library Cataloguing in Publication Data

Hooper, Anne
   Divorce and your children.
1. Divorce   2. Children of divorced parents
I. Title
306.8'9   HQ814
ISBN 0–04–649019–1

Set in 11 on 12 point Baskerville by Nene Phototypesetters, Northampton
and printed in Great Britain
by the Guernsey Press Co. Ltd, Guernsey, Channel Islands

To my extended family
To Phillip, Brian, Barnaby, Joel,
and Alexander

Acknowledgement

I'd like to thank the people who helped me with their advice and encouragement to complete this book. Many good wishes to Margaret Bramall, Elizabeth Muirhead, Ole Hansen of the Legal Action Group, Phillip Hodson, Nina West, Jackie Dineen, Catherine and Tim Harper, and Jane and Irene from Sidekicks who typed the manuscript.

Contents

Invitation

I'm hoping to follow up this book with a second one based on people's personal stories, the problems they had over divorce and the solutions they arrived at. Please write to me c/o Unwin Paperbacks, PO Box 18, Park Lane, Hemel Hempstead, Herts HP2 4TE and let me know what happened to you.

1

A Marriage
on the Rocks

John and Mary's marriage was foundering. They had been patching up their life together for the past year, but their frequent quarrels always tore holes in it again. When John found another partner, that spelt the end.

As in most divorces, feelings between the two of them were bitter. Their arguments became more and more dramatic and both became angry, hurt and vengeful. The one subject they did manage to agree on, however, was their children. Both cared for their son and daughter enormously and neither wanted the children to be hurt.

What was the best way to avoid hurting the kids? The answer seemed to be to seek help, professional help. 'Divorce counsellors will tell us what to do,' they reasoned. They managed to find a family psychiatric counsellor who proved very helpful when it came to clarifying their decisions about separation, but offered no information at all about their children's possible reaction. John and Mary had hoped for some kind of blueprint as to 'how to behave in divorce emergency', but they received none.

Their experience is probably familiar to many couples who do not know where to turn for advice. And, of course, thousands of other separating couples have never even heard of 'counsellors', and wouldn't know where to find one.

Suppose John and Mary *had* managed to find the right channels. What might they reasonably have expected?

Everyone's experience of divorce is unique, goes the argument. So how can you suggest one set of rules that will suit everyone?

You can't. But what you can do is to provide a solid basis of advice and information on which divorcing parents can draw. John and Mary's counsellor had done the best she could to help them as a couple. What she could also have described was how the majority of children react to various aspects of divorce. It sounds vague, written down here without detail, but this was the basic information John and Mary were seeking.

As John complained, 'Children, who should be the first people to be considered in a divorce, appear to be the last'.

At the moment, in Britain one out of four marriages end in divorce. If American statistics are anything to go by, it may soon become one in three. At present, 11 per cent of families are single-parent families, the majority of these being the product of divorce, and more than 1¼ million children are currently affected by divorce this year.

Three-quarters of all divorces involve children who are under sixteen, and yet there is no organization of any kind in Britain (except for small voluntary ones) which attempts to give the children of divorce a deal of their own.

The majority of divorces (46·3 per cent) occur in the first ten years of marriage, so that a considerable number of very young and particularly vulnerable children are affected. And the younger you are when you marry, the more likely you will be to divorce – which means that many parents who are themselves young, confused and inexperienced will be struggling in the dark, uncertain of how to cope.

You would think, bearing in mind the increasing number of divorced and separated households, that some research would have been done on the effects of divorce on children. A small amount has been carried out on children who have been the victims of marital disruption or breakdown. But virtually no research has ever been initiated in this country into discovering why many children survive divorce extremely well.

Perhaps the reason for this reluctance to investigate the state of divorce and its consequences lies in traditional attitudes towards divorce. Divorce is not only still unacceptable, it is *even now* frowned upon by certain arbiters of society. There are still organizations which, because of their obsession with the family as the keystone of society, are firmly opposed to anything, be it social or individual change, which attempts to cushion the impact of the break-up of a marriage, and so change the face of marital relationships. In our society, the family *is* the basis of both economic and, in the main, emotional welfare but, like any other social phenomenon, the family does have the ability to grow, develop and be flexible.

Historically, only those social structures that have been allowed to be flexible have survived. Because the family changes in size, shape and function, that does not mean we need expect the equivalent of the fall of the Roman Empire. (In contrast, there is an interesting incentive amongst consumer industries to *promote* divorce, because separating households means a demand for extra domestic appliances, furniture and so on).

More realistically, divorce may be looked on as another stage of 'growth', both in the life of the individuals concerned and in the metamorphosis of the social institution of marriage. In 1974 one in four marriages included a divorced person. Rather than expressing disillusionment with the wedded state, this indicates a real respect for the value of a happy wedded life.

But the survival of the old rigid idea 'once wedded, always wed' has made it exceedingly hard for couples to separate with dignity or to remain friends. Psychologically, we seem unable to acknowledge that divorce is here to stay. And since we have been slow to face up to the consequences of divorce, we have been unable to consider that there might be 'good' sides to it as well as 'bad'. The trouble is, if society acknowledges that 'once wedded, always wed' (which many people live with at great personal pain and expense) is a misconception, then society admits that it might have been wrong before, and no one likes doing that.

Meanwhile, back in the nursery, it is the children who suffer from these out-of-date ideas. Because their parents lack information and so are working in the dark, the children become the guinea-pigs who suffer from their mistakes. If the parents themselves feel they are doing something wrong by divorcing, how easily must the attitude of guilt and self-punishment filter down to the children.

The present stigma attached to divorce reminds me very

much of the old taboos surrounding birth control. In both cases, the children are the losers.

At this time of major upheaval children need support more than at any other. They need to feel they have a permanent base, they constantly need to keep in touch with familiar friends and relatives to provide them with reassurance that not *every* aspect of their life is changing. Divorce is a time when grandparents come into their own and when school provides the stability temporarily lacking at home.

The children need to be reassured that it is not their fault their parents are splitting up. They need to feel that *both* parents still love them, and they need to be introduced *gradually* to new step-parents and to be given a clear, truthful explanation about the state of play between Mum and Dad. If they are old enough to express them, their feelings should be discovered and given careful consideration when it comes to subjects such as access and custody.

The regular pattern of domestic life should be maintained if at all possible, as its familiarity provides a feeling of security. Above all, the absent parent must include them in his or her new life as a member of the family whenever they visit, and not treat them like guests at a birthday party.

Parents' respective roles have changed a lot during the last ten years, bringing the father much more actively into childcare. But it is still usually the wife who actually organizes family life. It is normally left to Mum to decide whether or not Joanna goes to play with Christina on Wednesdays, which friends to cultivate on Joanna's behalf and, once she is at school, how many friends and outside activities she can cope with on top of homework and the work and games she does at school.

It tends therefore to be tougher on fathers should they have custody (just under one-eighth of single-parent families are headed by fathers) because they know less about their children's regular social life and are not so used to planning it. They may not even know who their children's best friends are or where they live. Friends are one of the most valuable sources of support a 'divorced' child can have, and it cannot be emphasized too strongly how important it is for a child to keep in touch with them. This is particularly true of an only child, who has no brothers and sisters to help share the brunt of the break-up. Single children are the most vulnerable of all, and extra special thought and care needs to go into constructing a framework of emotional support, so that they suffer as little as possible.

When John and Mary first started off on their search for help, their aim was to avoid hurting the children or at least to make sure the children would be hurt 'as little as possible in the circumstances'. In some cases, the children may be hurt less by the divorce than by the marriage; for example, if one or other parent drinks heavily, or is violent or abusive. In other cases, one parent may be no more than a shadowy figure in the child's life, either through lack of parental interest or feeling, or because the economic facts of life dictate that he or she spends most of the time working away from home.

But even in the best handled separations the children usually do get hurt. They are frightened, anxious or upset because they love both parents, because they are used to both parents living together and because they no longer see as much of the absent parent as they want to. It is impossible to generalize about what is the most traumatic age for a child to lose a parent. It may be four, it may be fourteen. What *is* definite is that a child of any age needs a parent with a basic fund of knowledge about the child's own needs. Any parent, whether married happily or divorced, draws on such knowledge in order to provide a child with essential security, comfort and support.

The purpose of this book is to provide parents with the basic information they need in order to give a child making the journey through divorce the right kind of mental, emotional and social support. In this way, it is possible to minimize or at least to reduce, the amount of suffering they experience. And by helping their children, parents may end up helping themselves too.

2

Separation — Step by Step

Most people go into marriage with every intention of staying married for ever, so the fateful day of marital breakdown finds them in a state of shock, totally unprepared for what is happening. For the reasons outlined in the first chapter, there is still a taboo on accepting divorce as an everyday reality. After all, runs the head-in-the-sand argument, if we go into marriage thinking it won't last, it is much more likely to disintegrate eventually. 'Anyway,' we all say, 'it's not going to happen to us,' and the unpalatable subject is quickly dismissed.

Because people think it is not going to happen to them, not only is the individual left feeling extremely vulnerable when the worst happens, but society as a whole is not geared towards dealing with such crises. The *only* system of advice set up in this country to deal specifically with divorce is the legal system. There is no emotional counselling immediately and easily accessible, no crisis centres have been established and, so far, there is surprisingly little media information. The law, although it is now very much concerned with making financial provision for children, was originally established to safeguard the financial rights of *parents*. Often, when it is interpreted in the extreme — as many solicitors insist on doing to safeguard themselves from accusations of *not* acting in their client's best interest — such hard feelings develop between the parents that the children's distress is magnified a hundredfold. So, at present, it is impossible to paint anything other than a gloomy picture of the amount of divorce support available.

All this means only one thing – self-help. If there are no 'divorce organizations' to help us, we must help ourselves. We therefore need to equip ourselves with as much information as possible, so that right from the beginning of the crisis we can act in the best possible way for our children.

1 TAKING TIME OVER SEPARATION

Although the world seems to be coming to an end right now, it will probably survive till next week. During that time a couple can do their best to make preparation and provision for themselves and their children. Even if it takes as much as one month or three to make the actual break, that's all right. There is no rule to say one partner is forced to move away from home the minute a couple decide to separate – because the partner doesn't leave immediately, it doesn't mean the departure will never happen. It indicates rather that they are mature people taking a great deal of care over one of the most important decisions of a lifetime. Don't let anyone tell you anything different and don't let any friend, relation or (particularly) lover hustle you away from your family until you feel sure you have made reasonable preparation for your departure.

2 REASSURE YOUR CHILDREN

Children will realize something disturbing is going on even if they don't know what it is. If they are very young, they may show their unease by becoming very difficult and tearful. When you too are feeling difficult and tearful it is hard to cope with an extra emotional burden. Remember that you are *all* suffering, so try to be extra nice to them.

3 SEEK PROFESSIONAL ADVICE FOR EMOTIONAL PROBLEMS

It is *not* an admission of failure to seek professional advice on how best to behave towards your children. I strongly recommend seeking counselling *before* you actually separate, rather than waiting for your children to show signs of distress because it is often the way in which the divorce is handled and explained that has sparked off their uncertainties and consequent misery. After all, prevention is better than cure.

Although there are no national 'divorce counselling' organizations, there are a variety of people who can be of assistance. They will not all be able to help and you may have to appeal to some of them on a 'crisis' basis to evoke their sympathies. Individual people and organizations vary from district to district. A certain GP may be a wonderful divorce adviser, while another may lack the time or experience to help. You may be able to walk into some places off the street and get advice, while others will insist on your being referred by a GP or a social worker.

(a) **The National Marriage Guidance Council** (you can find your local branch in the telephone directory). Marriage guidance counsellors can be extremely useful in allowing you to work out your own ideas of how to handle the situation but they are not allowed to come up with specific suggestions or advice.

(b) **The Citizens Advice Bureau** does *not* give counselling but may be able to send you directly to someone who can. But it does supply information, and can put you in touch with appropriate counsellors and advisors.

(c) **Local authorities** do not offer counselling as such but social workers come into contact with all kinds of emotional and social problems every day, usually at crisis level. Some social workers are very receptive to the idea of working to help prevent tragedies, rather than only being invited in after the event. Social workers in country districts tend to have more time to do this than those in towns.

How to get in touch with your social worker. Telephone the social services department of your local authority (they will be in the telephone directory). Ask for the duty officer. When you have explained the problem, you will be put through to the social worker who deals with people from your specific area. If he or she agrees to see you, it will be this person who from now on is assigned to you and your family. In some places it may be more effective to walk into the local social security offices and ask to see the duty officer. If you explain that you are in the middle of a crisis and need help *now*, the immediacy of your appeal may produce more helpful results than a phone call would.

(d) It may be that the social worker will refer you elsewhere, to a person or group that would be better equipped to help you. One of these resources might be the local **Child Guidance Clinic.** These clinics exist to give family counselling to parents and children and some of them will accept you as a client without any referral from a third party. Others will insist you come through a GP or a social worker.

(e) If you live in a big city district, there may be a special centre or institute for **Family and Child Guidance.** The local Citizens Advice Bureau should be able to give you details about it and tell you where to find it.

(f) Your local **probation office** includes, amongst all its other schemes for family help, a marital/divorce counselling service. So far this has tended to be used only when there is a dispute over access to a child before, during or after divorce. And although, in theory, probationary help should be available to anyone divorcing, in practice it is not always possible to get it. The local authority headquarters or the Citizens Advice Bureau will advise you where the local probation office is and how you can approach them. Whether or not the probation officer will agree to help with divorce counselling *before* there is disagreement remains to be seen. At least, it is certainly a resource worth testing.

(g) There is a central British Organization called the **British Association of Counselling,** 1a Little Church Street, Rugby (Rugby (0788) 78328), which has a register of names and addresses of all small groups, clinics and organizations providing counselling in aspects of divorce, family therapy and children's welfare. You can find out from them whether there are any such practitioners in your area. These organizations mostly work on a fee-paying basis, although many of them operate a sliding scale of fees and some are funded by church or charitable institutions.

(h) If there is nothing in the way of counselling in your area, or if what there is proves unsatisfactory, the self-help association **Gingerbread** has social groups in most areas, and you may be able to get help here. Gingerbread does not provide counselling, but operates on a social level (see Chapter 5). But as most of its members have been through divorce, there may well be people in a local group who would be prepared to talk to you about their experiences and how they coped. Gingerbread groups advertise in local newspapers. If you don't see their name appearing in the small ads column, you can ring the Gingerbread central office at 35 Wellington Street, London WC2 (01-240 0953).

(i) Some **state schools** have a social worker attached to them who may volunteer advice if asked. Certainly you should inform the social worker about your separation, ask him to keep an eye on your children and to tell you if they show signs of distress or behaviour that is out of character. Of course, if this should happen, it would be wise to ask his advice on the best way to deal with it. You should also tell the head teacher and the class teacher of your separation and ask them to look out for signs of unhappiness.

(j) If you can afford private help, your GP may be able to recommend a **private child psychologist** or **psychiatrist**.

(k) The recent success of a divorce conciliation project in Bristol has inspired many other probation offices and independent groups to open similar services. The **Bristol Courts Family Conciliation Council for Voluntary Service**, 9 Elmdale Road, Bristol, aims to help divorcing parents deal with custody and access problems at an early stage, with as little ill-feeling as possible. Addresses for other local **conciliation services** may be obtained from local probation offices or the local **Citizens Advice Bureau** (see telephone directory).

An offshoot of conciliation work has been the growth of **divorce experience groups**. Run by local probation offices in Leicester, Birmingham, Edinburgh, Chesterfield and Lincoln, these groups advise divorcing parents and provide psychological and legal information. Addresses available from local probation offices.

I am not suggesting you should intensively research every one of the avenues mentioned above. But constructive talk with one knowledgeable person will help you straighten out the best course of action for *you* to take with your particular family. Sadly, it is not easy to find divorce counselling, hence the list of every possible source.

Advice on problems other than emotional ones, such as finance or housing, can be found in Chapter 5.

How to Use a Counsellor

Talk through the situation, working out the best way to discuss the divorce with the children. If possible go through a 'dummy run' before you actually talk to the children. If you can arrange it, go back to the counsellor *after* you have broken the news, with feedback on how the children have reacted, so that you can prepare yourself to cope during the next few weeks. It may be that several visits during the early weeks of separation will help you work out how best to cope with your own emotions and your children's. The counsellor may also wish to include the children in some or all of these sessions.

4   DO-IT-YOURSELF COUNSELLING

Not everyone is going to want to consult a counsellor, however. Some people may not have the time to do so. Others may believe strongly that divorce is something very personal, to be kept strictly within the family, and that any discussion should be between the separating partners only. There are people who think (erroneously, in my opinion) that counsellors make emotional crises worse rather than better.

What kind of questions should these parents ask themselves before approaching their offspring? The important one is, 'What will our children need the most reassurance about?' If you can sort out some of the details of how your separation is going to affect their lives, it would be sensible to do so. Try to work out a simple explanation of why you are separating.

5 TELLING THE CHILDREN

It is important to tell the children the news yourselves and to do so before anyone else (relative, neighbour) says the wrong thing at the wrong time in front of them.

It is also vital to be honest, and *not* to hide any of the relevant facts – for example, that one parent has already left home. When parents avoid talking about their separation, the children's fears are magnified and they replace reality with fantasy and imaginary defences. Over-protection can hurt them. It is often easier for them to face a painful reality than an anguished uncertainty.

It is also desirable for both parents to tell the children *together*, however hard this may be. If both parents are there, it is easier to avoid putting all the blame on to one or the other. And it is better for the children, because it means they do not have to take sides. The more conflict that emerges in telling the children the sad tale, the more insecure they will feel. The conversation should therefore be held, if possible, during an emotional lull in the separation. If it is held immediately after a bitter argument, the details will emerge in an angrier way and so will hurt and confuse.

The most important reassurance of all – and this needs to be stressed over and over again – is that you *both* love the children. *Just because you no longer love each other, this does not mean that you don't love them.* You do. It is a *vital* message which must be got across.

What each child will want to know varies from one individual to another. It is certainly a good idea to work out some details of your proposed new lifestyle if you can. After all, *your* life is going to affect theirs.

If the kids are through the toddler stage they are going to want to know what will happen to them. Who will they live with? Will their toys go with them? Are they going to move house? District? Even country? Will school be changed? Who will look after them? Will they still have the same old friends? If the children are older, they may want to know more about the social implications. Are the relatives going to think badly of them? Will they become curiosities at school?

How to Break the News

Explain that you are not happy living together and therefore you are going to live apart; that you will both cheer up and become happier people when this happens, even if it takes a while. If you have been having a lot of distressing rows, you could say, 'I expect you've noticed we haven't been very happy lately'.

It is not necessary to go into details about the rows. Too much detail can be confusing for young children, although older children may *want* to know. Many children may already be upset and confused from overhearing the fights. When they ask specific questions, they should be given specific answers, although not a list of every single accusation or blow-by-blow account of your quarrels. Rather than describing how Daddy has victimized Mummy over spending money on her clothes and how Mummy has run Daddy into the ground with her avaricious demands, it is quite enough to say simply that you have found it impossible to agree over money and your disagreements are now so strong that it has become impossible to live happily together any more.

To the parents, immersed in one of the most traumatic upheavals of their lives, these disputes seem of paramount importance. And so they are, but *only to them*. The quarrels which loom so large in their lives are irrelevant to anyone else. That includes the children.

6 THE CHILDREN'S REACTION

Expect to be asked the same questions over and over again. This may not happen when you first break the news, but is bound to during the consecutive weeks. It is very hard for anyone to take in the fact that two people are divorcing. The children's need for repeated explanations is their method of coping with and working through the perplexing situation (see Chapter 3 for more detail on this point). Be prepared to give your explanations time and again.

A good way in which to tell something distressing is to hold your children very closely while you talk. Your body warmth will do a lot to reassure them and show them that they are not being abandoned. This practice will help reassure a child of *any* age, although some people may find this hard to believe and even harder to do.

If your children cry, don't try to make them stop, or tell them 'to be brave'. Crying is good for them – it is natural expression of their grief. If you teach them to bottle up their feelings and repress grief, they may later find release in an explosion that could be very harmful.

If the children appear to have little or no reaction to your news, don't be too surprised. It may mean they have not yet had time to feel the impact of what they have just been told. It is often the questions they ask during the next weeks that are more telling.

One common reaction is that the children think they have somehow managed to cause the divorce. Their experiences have taught them that when they are good they are rewarded, and when they are bad they are punished. Divorce can therefore seem like a retribution. The children may search their minds for something 'wicked' they have done which they feel has caused the split. For example, one girl remembered a time in the past when she and her brother had been particularly noisy. Their father, in a fit of annoyance, had yelled at her that he couldn't stand it when she fought with her brother. She was later convinced it was because she had carried on fighting after being asked not to that her father had been driven away from home.

Often these feelings of childish guilt may seem inexplicable and unreasonable to parents, who will be inclined to dismiss them. But they are real enough to the children, which is why the mother and father should repeat to their offspring over and over again that they are unhappy with each other, *not* with the children.

When Bob and Rosemary told their two sons, aged six and four, that they were going to live in separate houses, they explained they were no longer happy living together and felt they would be better living apart. The eldest child burst into tears briefly and asked, 'Where will Mummy go to?' When it was explained that Daddy was the one who was departing, not Mummy, he stopped crying. The youngest child showed no immediate reaction to this news. He hadn't really understood what it meant. Both parents emphasized to the children how much they loved them and how Daddy would see them very often. They had taken the precaution of inviting two young cousins to stay for the weekend to act as a diversion from the unhappiness of the grown-ups and also to act as confidantes should the boys need someone to talk to.

In contrast, Sharon and Roger dragged out continual bouts of argument and weeping which culminated in Roger leaving the house, declaring he could not stay there a minute longer. It was left to a heartbroken Sharon, who hadn't wanted Roger to go, to break the news to three-year-old Samantha. She managed this between fits of crying, and was so distraught she could hardly speak. Not surprisingly, Samantha quickly formed the idea that Daddy had left them completely alone, that he didn't love them, and that Mummy was so upset she wasn't able to look after Samantha very well.

This last conclusion made Samantha feel very insecure indeed for, in the event of losing one parent, she badly needed the remaining one to be strong.

For three months Samantha didn't see her father again because he thought that a clean break would be better for all of them. The love and support he could have shown to his daughter was therefore never demonstrated. When Roger visited his family at Christmas time, his fears about reopening the wound seemed to be confirmed as his presence did trigger off painful memories of desertion in the minds of his wife and daughter. Samantha was particularly confused: she was pleased to see her Daddy but upset by her mother's distress.

Roger departed convinced he had made the wrong move and did not visit again for a long time. Three months, six months is a very long absence in a little girl's life and, in this case, was sadly unnecessary. Sharon's distress could easily have been bypassed by Roger arranging to see Samantha when Sharon was not there. This way, the adults' pain would have had a chance to die down while Samantha continued a valuable relationship with the Daddy she loved.

The value of the 'extended family' is obvious here. If there had been a friend or relative, a brother or sister, to help buffer the upset, Samantha would have found the transition of separation much easier (see Chapter 8 on the

New Extended Family and Step-parents).

Compare Roger's abrupt departure and disturbed little girl with Bob and Rosemary's cheerful and sensible boys. When Bob left, it was to go to a tiny flat. He didn't 'just walk out'. Instead, he took his time (over three weeks) about making all necessary and practical arrangements. After he had gone, Rosemary arranged that she either left the house when Bob came round or that the kids went out with him to his new home or to his mother's house. They managed to organize things so that Bob saw almost as much of them as before, but he still managed to steer clear of Rosemary. They thus minimized the amount of hurt involved in contact with each other. Every change they made was carefully and clearly explained to the children, who were included in Rosemary and Bob's new plans as much as they had been in family plans in the past.

Shelley and Jim are a young separated couple with an eight-year-old son, Tom. Their break-up had been quite amicable and both had managed to fix themselves up with homes. Shelley stayed on in their flat with Tom, and began to retrain so that she would eventually be able to earn a living. Jim moved into a big rundown house which he shared with six other people. This house was filled with a variety of ever-changing friends. Shelley was delighted for Tom to go to his father every weekend and, on the face of it, things seemed well thought-out.

After about four months, though, Tom's grandmother became increasingly worried about the child because he had taken to literally tearing his hair out. When she mentioned this to Shelley, she was laughed at for being a fusspot. But eventually Shelley could not fail to see that her mother was right. At her mother's insistence, the family discussed the problem with the local social worker, who referred the family to a child guidance clinic.

Although Shelley and Jim had already lived apart for a while, they agreed that they and Tom should all see the child guidance worker together. What emerged from their talks was that neither of them had explained what they were doing, and why, to their son. Nor had his mother's enthusiasm for her new training and his father's reversion to life as a single really left any space for an eight-year-old.

What both had considered to be the behaviour of a tiresome

little boy turned out to be Tom's way of saying that he didn't want to bunk down on the floor of his father's room every Saturday night in a confusing and noisy household, that he did not want to spend an entire weekend away from everything familiar and home-like, and that on the short times he and his mother were together he wanted her to behave like a mother instead of a career girl.

It had never occurred to Shelley and Jim that they should talk about their plans for separation to Tom. Nor had it occurred to them them that their child had needs which could have been expressed during this communication and which should *also* have been taken into account when separating. It is often difficult to see your child as a human being separate from yourself.

Shelley *did* have to learn how to earn a living, and Jim *could* only afford to live in a rundown house resembling a squat. They had assumed Tom would fall in with their plans because there didn't seem to be any alternative. But both these necessities could have been amended to take Tom's welfare into consideration – which is what eventually happened.

Tom spent more time with his mother, time which she was able to plan around him. Both she and Jim helped Tom build up a circle of friends who were welcome in either home. On the now occasional times he stayed at his father's house, a proper bed was provided in Jim's room and next to it a shelf had been designated for Tom's belongings only. A space had been made for his life amongst theirs, a space which should have been provided from the start.

These three examples illustrate how the main steps of separation can constructively help and support the children: the steps of (1) constantly reassuring them you *both* love them; (2) informing them clearly but without 'overload' about what is happening; and (3) planning the future taking them realistically into account.

It is no accident that, in setting out these 'rules', the emphasis has been on explaining *together*, arranging the children's access to *both* of you. The reasons for this are enlarged on in Chapter 3.

But it can't always be done like that, can it? Often you can't predict the blazing temper or the traumatic sorrow which decides what kind of a separation is on the cards? It isn't always possible to channel your emotions into a nice, friendly split, but it still helps to possess certain knowledge. Even if you do slam the door behind you after an appalling row, your passionate behaviour doesn't change the fact that a certain combination of childcare is likely to benefit everyone in the long run. If you are aware of this you have already gone part of the way towards altering your behaviour during the split.

Often the effects of divorce are so upsetting that you are incapable of doing anything rational. 'I was feeling so terrible,' said Dinah, 'that I couldn't be strong and supportive to my kids.' Fair enough, but you can still pick up the phone and ask someone else to come round and help out. This is the time to call on friends, relations, neighbours, anyone who can help, especially with the children's sorrows. This is the time to make sure the children see as much of their friends as possible, because those friends will give them a sense of support and belonging. But, above all, the most important thing to realize is that a child needs two-parents, even if they no longer need each other.

3

Your Children Need You Both

I am not of the school that says when a parent leaves the marital home he/she should disappear completely from the children's lives because *this is what is best for the children.* Anyone who encourages that course of non-action (usually the embittered parent who remains in charge of the children) is inviting the possibility of long-term distress. Witness the 32-year-old woman whose mother deserted her when she was three, cutting out of Margaret's life as if she had never existed. Except that she had existed and twenty-nine years later her daughter' was suffering from continual feelings of depression and inability to keep any love relationship going for longer than two years, due to an overriding feeling of inadequacy. 'Why did my mother desert me?' she must have asked herself time and again during childhood. Because, comes the childish answer, there is something badly wrong with me. However much a 32-year-old can appreciate the irrationality of it, beneath the surface the desolate child is emotionally still reliving the desertion.

Not every child who never sees one of its parents again is going to react with such pain. But it is easy to see that when one of the most important people in your life apparently fails to take the trouble to communicate with you (and therefore, in the youngster's brain, has stopped caring), you feel let down and inadequate, and begin to lack confidence.

It is interesting that a persistent need to know one's background, a need to fill in the blank patches in one's life, has prompted enough political pressure in England to bring about adoption reform which now allows adopted children to identify their natural parents. If it is recognized that there is such a mental need on the part of those deserted children, why should this not hold good for those children who lose only one parent?

Step-parents can, to some extent, fill the gap (see Chapter 8) but what step-parents don't have is that inherited background that we share with a natural parent. Through our genes we inherit certain physical features of our parents. There is an anthropological theory that we also inherit certain mental characteristics – such as, for example, a tendency to be quick-tempered. It is because of these inherited tendencies that we are likely to respond and thrive more fully in our own family than in someone else's. Even if the theory of inherited mental characteristics turns out to be incorrect, by the time we have spent some years with a parent, we will be so conditioned to fit in with his or her life patterns that it will naturally be easier to live with and to learn from natural parents than from step- or foster-parents.

And one parent is a historic gateway to all of his or her own family, so the loss of a parent can mean the loss of a whole set of interesting relations. I take after my maternal uncle who was looked on as a black sheep of his family because *he* had the temerity to get divorced. As a little girl I used to admire his buoyancy in spite of knowing that he was not really approved of. When I had done something naughty, I felt a bit better for it, just thinking about him.

On a different tack, I loved hearing about my maternal grandmother's family. My Victorian great-grandfather was a rogue who married my maternal grandmother mainly for her Welsh inheritance. My grandmother's brothers, who had exotic names like Herman, Horatio and Nelson, roamed the world doing exciting things from running fish and chip parlours in Great Yarmouth to copper mining in South Africa. If my Mum had left me as a kid, I would never have known these things. Of course I would have survived and of course materially they would not have mattered at all. But I feel as though some of their buccaneering attitudes have rubbed off on me, just through blood association, and I feel good about them. They help give me my identity. It is probably for this sort of reason that some people go to great trouble and expense to try and unearth details about their ancestors.

It's a common experience in marriage counselling and sex therapy to find that the patient comes, not necessarily from a disturbed background, but often from one where a parent (usually, but not always, the father) is either physically absent or, although actually in the home, mentally absent. That is, he never takes a part in his children's life. Swedish and American studies have shown that contact with the father after divorce is important, especially for boys, and that irregular or no visiting leads to poor adjustment in later life.

An interesting common factor in the lives of women who are unable to respond satisfactorily sexually is a type of isolation experienced as a teenager. Often these women have not had parents they could talk to easily, nor did they find it easy to make friends at school. Being 'alone' during the vulnerable time of puberty often means that there will be sex problems and a lack of communication during married life. Recent British research suggests, too, that separation from the father before a girl reaches the age of eleven may badly affect her later adjustment to motherhood.

I am mentioning these long-term problems as further fuel for my strongly-held belief that the departed parent should be encouraged to keep up active contact with his or her children.

KEEPING IN TOUCH

So what about the argument that says the children will be painfully affected when they see a parent intermittently after they have been used to seeing him or her for most of the time? Even if this point is valid, think how much *worse* it is going to be if the children don't see the parent at all. Instead of going through a period of occasional pain on meeting and parting – which they will get used to and eventually get over because they know, by the continued meetings, that the departed parent *does* care for them – they may endure the utter trauma of feeling deserted.

Split loyalties are inevitable. But there are unhappy split loyalties and much better balanced ones, depending on how the parents handle discussion about each other.

But children are immensely adaptable. As long as they *know* Daddy or Mummy will always spend regular time with them, they will learn to take the new arrangements in their stride. It is important to emphasize that the departed parent *must* be consistent about his access, must be on time and must *never* forget meetings or cancel them at the last minute. It is when the parent becomes unreliable and breaks promises that the children can't rely on him and consequently feel bad.

Very often there are physical reasons which make it difficult for a parent to see the children (he is in Bristol and they are in London, say). But it is still possible to keep in touch, by telephoning, writing, sending presents, however small – all constant reminders that the children are still cherished.

I believe it is important to keep in touch, even if it is over a long distance. During the last war there were many toddlers who had never met their fathers. But those whose mothers constantly talked about the father had a picture of him in their heads, so that when Dad returned he wasn't a complete stranger. There were already bonds of affection created for him and he had a place in their life. It managed to seem quite normal to have a 'new daddy' move in.

If you contrast these experiences with those of a woman whose father was killed in the war, and who had *never* heard anything about him from the mother, it is not difficult to understand her unhappy childhood.

'I felt isolated from other children. They would play games like mums and dads at my elementary school and I didn't know how to join in. I can understand why my mother hardly ever mentioned my father, but I think now she was wrong. All I knew as a kiddie was that I was different, and I hated it. I wanted to be exactly the same as all the others.

'As a little girl I became embarrassingly attached to a male teacher – embarrassing, that was, to the teacher. I was not-very-gently dissuaded from my yearnings for him.

'I was only six and I had dreamt up a whole romantic passion about him. I see now I was trying to give myself a father in the only way my little brain could think of. Not being allowed to show love for this man made everything far worse. I got over it, of course; one gets over everything. But I found, when I reached my twenties, that I was terrified of young men laughing at me –

so scared that it was a long time before I got up the strength to go out with anyone. The man I married really only succeeded with me by being very persistent – he had to be, otherwise I would never have believed he really wanted me. Thinking back on it now, I can't understand why he persevered. I was impossible.'

Much of the children's distress stems *not* from the actual separation but from the disturbance they have been experiencing during the previous months or years of their parents' unhappiness. Once the quarrels and discord are removed from the home, they are likely to be far happier, or at least are given the opportunity to mentally recuperate.

What you do have to arrange, though, is for your partner to see the children without having to see you. This way, both you and the kids are spared the flare-ups of anger that are easily sparked off simply by meeting. Better to confine your fights to privacy or to the telephone. If your partner sees the children after school, let him pick them up directly from the school. If they are collected at the weekend, try and arrange for a friend to hand them over at pick-up time. If you are lucky enough to have an *au pair* or a babyminder, let her be the go-between. If Grandma lives on the premises, let her do the exchange. Ask your spouse to make similar arrangements.

None of these problems is an argument for one of you to drop out of the children's life completely. But attending to them ensures that *when* you see your offspring, you do so regularly and consistently, preferably without being in contact with your spouse, in order to avoid war.

TAKING SIDES

It is easy for the parents to confuse *their* feelings of pain, when they see one another after separation, with their children's distress. Don't expect the children to automatically take sides. Your argument about not living together is not their's. They have a wholly separate viewpoint. Don't assume that, because *you* can't stand the sight of your partner, the same applies to your kids. And try to bear in mind that, even though you wish your spouse would disappear off the face of the earth, your children will probably want to stay in contact, even more than they did before. So, if you are the parent in charge of the family, don't make the mistake of banning your ex-spouse from the children. In a couple of years, your grief and rage will have died down, and you will be able to see clearly that the children never ever shared the same rage.

UNDESIRABLE INFLUENCE

It is also easy for the parent with care to argue that the deserting partner is an undesirable influence and therefore might be harmful in shaping the character of your mutual progeny. Except in the most extreme cases of child and wife battering, this argument is highly suspect.

Even the most unpleasant alcoholic husband can be a sympathetic and caring father. The frigid and chronically neurotic wife can be a warm and loving mum. The fact is that for every undesirable characteristic your erstwhile spouse displays, there is a redeeming one. By the time you have reached divorce point, his or her attractive side will have become a thing of the past, *for you*, but not necessarily for your infants. The world is made up of people who are not perfect, just like your spouse. And the sooner your children learn to cope with the difficulties displayed by human nature (and where better to start than at home), the easier they will find it to become mature and caring adults themselves.

It does not follow that, because Johnny's daddy is obsessive about keeping house to the point of fining Johnny's mummy every time she accidentally runs out of milk, Johnny will grow up to browbeat his wife in exactly the same way if he has regular access to his father as a child. For Johnny has a choice of behaviours to learn from. Not only does he receive mental instruction from his parents, but there are also his grandparents, family friends, babyminder, *au pair*, outsiders, and so on.

As he learns that there are some kinds of behaviour that Granny does not like but which his mother could not care less about, he learns to adjust his behaviour accordingly. And in later life, the computer which is his brain will sort through the different types of censure, approval and resulting behaviours and will choose the ones that fit best into the pattern of his personality. Hopefully, it will be Dad's loving nursing of Johnny during the weekends he is suffering from chicken-pox which will leave a positive imprint in his memory, rather than Dad's tetchy discipline.

BETTER OFF WITHOUT HIM

I have often heard my divorced friends say, 'I've managed perfectly all right without him/her', 'I reckon we're better off without'. What they mean is that they as the parents are better off. But their children are not. As I have said, I believe that except in a few circumstances where to see a departed parent would be detrimental to the children's development, they still need that other parent's influence.

We all learn as children, not just from what our mothers and fathers tell us, but from what they do, how they do it, and how they react. We discover that their reactions and attitudes differ according to whom they are with. For example, Mummy is flirtatious with the milkman, cross with Daddy and her face lights up when she looks at the baby. We also discover that whereas Mummy is flirtatious with the milkman, Daddy doesn't pay any attention to him but is very lively when the pretty woman who lives next door comes round. Similarly, Daddy loves football while Mummy can't imagine what he sees in it.

So we unconsciously drink in different sets of values from each parent. We would therefore lack the masculine values if Daddy disappeared from the scene and the feminine ones if Mummy were never at home again.

RULES FOR SINGLE PARENTS

Perhaps, though, the situation is outside your control, and your spouse has done a flit from the domestic scene, never to return. What do you do then? Willy-nilly, your children *have* got an absent parent.

Rule 1. However tempting it may be, don't run your partner down. It hurts the kids to think that their mother or their father is a swine. There is plenty of time later on for them to work that out for themselves. It is also possible that, given time, your spouse may change his mind about cutting ties with parenthood, will realize that he has made a mistake and want to make up for it. All the more reason not to have poisoned Junior's mind. Separation is a very easy time to make mistakes.

Rule 2. It is important for your children to have a clear image of the absent parent. Angela, aged six, developed a fantasy friend two years after her father had left for good. It is quite common for children to have fantasy friends but Angela told her mother that this friend was Daddy. Daddy, it seemed, was always with Angela wherever she went. If she got into any trouble, Daddy, rather like Superman, would swoop down and rescue her. She would pretend to read invisible letters from this Daddy, who would go away on his travels a lot. He would usually be writing from a far-away place over the sea, and the boat trip there and back took such a long time that this was why they hadn't seen him for ages. Starved of information about her father, Angela had needed to invent him.

Talking matter-of-factly about your ex-partner, what he/she used to do, what his/her favourite television programme was, how he/she used to hate soap getting in his/her eyes at bathtime just like Junior does, all helps to build up a realistic picture of Dad/Mum which is very necessary for your children's mental growth. By feeding them constant information about your partner, you are helping to make those children feel whole.

Rule 3. If Dad is the one who has left, encourage male friends, brothers or your father to spend regular time in your home. Of course, they won't be the same as Dad, but they will help. Conversely, if Mum is the departed one, encourage your mother, or your sisters, or a housekeeper, to take an active part in your lives.

In California, there are kindergarten schools where all the helpers and teachers are men. Ninety per cent of the children attending this school come from single-parent families, most of them living with their mother. The theory behind the all-male staff is that they will provide a masculine aspect to the children's lives which would otherwise be lacking. In England, male participation in the lives of very young children is still a novel idea. There are some individual branches of Gingerbread (see Chapter 5) which make this provision for children in their play schemes. Often childcare duties in the Gingerbread play schemes are shared by both males and females.

Parents of older children could encourage them to share in spare-time activities where they'll meet both sexes, such as a youth club or similar sort of organization if that appeals to them. Camping holidays with other people outside the family might be a way of helping them to make new friends of both sexes who could help to give them the masculine or femine influence they are lacking.

OLDER CHILDREN

So far in this chapter I have been talking about younger children, up to the age of about six. But most of the suggestions I have made hold good for all age groups. The principle of the children needing both parents is just as true when they are older. But as the children grow up, they become more independent and develop a mental and a social life of their own. Their needs are different, their tastes are more developed, they have activities which demand time of their own.

DIFFERENT AGE GROUPS

Eight-year-olds
At around the age of eight, for example, children go through a period of rapid mental growth. A lot can change. Jim, who for years had spent his time being physically very active (he would build with Lego, draw innumerable pictures, thump his younger brother, play exceedingly rough games with his friends, and watch television avidly) suddenly discovered reading. Every evening after school he used to retire to his bedroom at the top of the house where he would cram his head full of the exploits of comic book heroes, adventure stories and children's detective thrillers. He had gone from being a rather bored television viewer to total involvement in every story book he could lay hands on.

His mother, who had based a great part of their time together on creating active things for Jim to do during her weekend access, suddenly found she had time on her hands. Instead of insisting, on one occasion, that he helped her bake a cake he had especially asked to make previously, she simply gave him the opportunity to do so. When he refused, she didn't push the baking any further. She knew that if she forced her presence on him when he was so stimulated by something new, he would feel frustrated and resentful.

Need for Privacy. Everybody needs privacy, and that includes children. The parent who has left often finds that on his/her days for having the children, he/she is in an artificial situation, where it is quite hard to behave normally. Before leaving Jim's father, Jim's mother found it no great sweat to let Jim get on with his own thing if he wanted to. But she valued Jim's presence so much during the smaller amount of time she subsequently was able to spend with him that she had grown used to making every activity with him count. So it was hard for her to realize that Jim no longer wanted the intense activity she had been used to organizing for him.

Twelve-year-olds

And as the children grow older, this need for time and space grows too. Sarah's father used to find that the best way to make twelve-year-old Sarah feel at home with him at the weekends was for her to know that she had her own place in his house. She had her own room, her own books and a record player. Her friends were as welcome in his house as they were in her mother's home, and he was able to accept that for a large part of their weekends together he might not see her, because she was so busy with the friends.

One of my mother's complaints about me as I grew older was that I tended to treat our home as a hotel. I can appreciate now that this must be tough on the parent who has been so bound up in caring for you all those years. But what I can also remember is that urgent need to do things on my own during my teenage years. Even when the children's time is divided between two homes, the same rules still apply. Children of divorce also need independence.

I also think that from around the age of ten the children's wishes about the amount of time they spend in either household should be taken into account. I am not recommending that every time they voice a wish it should be granted. But I think they should actually be asked what they prefer, and that subsequent arrangements between parents should allow them to feel they have had some choice about what is, after all, their life. Children should not be forced to see the other parent if they feel strongly that they don't want to. The other parent mustn't lose heart should this happen, though. Children do change!

APART FOR EVER

The younger the children are, the less likely they are to accept that you and your partner are going to be apart forever. Forever is such a huge concept in a youngster's head that it is meaningless and frightening at the same time. The younger the children are, the more they are likely to persist in their hopes that one day Mummy and Daddy will come back to live together again. Which may mean they will be continuously pressing you to do so and will create avid fantasies about these possibilities. Try not to get irritated. They can't help it; indeed they probably need the fantasies in order to feel better.

As they grow older, they will still have them but they will also have a more mature over-knowledge that although dreams would be nice as reality, they *are* only dreams.

SIGNS OF DISTURBANCE

Disturbance can begin at any age but children from the age of eight upwards seem especially vulnerable.[1] Perhaps this is because eight is the age when a child is mature enough to be able to reason about the divorce but young enough to get those reasons very confused. Boys are seemingly more likely to be upset by divorce and separation than girls are.[2]

[1] *US Journal of Clinical Child Psychology, Vol. VI, No. 2, Divorce: Its Impact Upon Children and Youth.* Published by the American psychological Association, 1100 NE 13th, Oklahoma City, Oklahoma 73117, USA. The most compact and complete collection of American research papers on the subject of children and divorce.

[2] *Parent–Child Separation.* Michael Rutter, pp 233–260. Journal of Child Psychology and Psychiatry. Vol. 12, 1971. Pergamon Press.

A disturbed child shows special signs of distress such as depression, when he may be quiet, withdrawn, sleep a lot, or be totally listless and lacking in enthusiasm. He may wet his bed, be aggressive, bully other children, and so on. Children of divorce often need extra love and reassurance. When Jane starts attacking every child in the playground, what she might be trying to get across is, 'Reassure me. Tell me that you love me. Tell me I'm all right.' It is important that *both* parents make it clear to her that they do love her, that they are always going to love her and that their love for her is not going to change. Some disturbance at the beginning of divorce is natural but it is only if the symptoms persist over a long period – say, for more than nine months – that it would be wise to seek professional advice.

MAKING A PACT WITH YOUR PARTNER

It is worth trying to make a pact with your partner that, however much you may be trying to cut each other's throats over all other aspects of splitting up, when it comes to your children's welfare, you stick to the same stories and give the same explanations. It is very easy to use your children as weapons against each other, and the most well-meaning parents sometimes do so (see Chapter 6). So it helps the situation to work out how you are going to handle the children and then stick to your plans.

'What upset me most,' says Kate, who was six when her parents separated and is now twenty, 'were the totally different stories they would tell me about the same thing. After all, if one of them was telling the truth, it meant the other was lying his or her head off, and that really hurt. My childhood was spent in painful confusion and in fact I've blotted out most of it, as a mental self-defence. Because I never knew who to believe, I didn't have any firm ground to stand on in my beliefs, and I became very uncertain about myself and everything around me. At my primary school I was very isolated and miserable. I had no friends at all.

'My secondary school was better. I did make friends there but I was always the one who was different. I'd been through so many of my parents' battles that I ended up very old for my age.

I started sleeping around when I was fourteen. I mean being really promiscuous. I got quite a name for it. I think I must have been seeking some kind of emotional reassurance, which I didn't get. In three years of sleeping around I never had a steady relationship. Finally, though, I met Jock who had had a childhood that was even more unhappy than mine. He'd also had a traumatic infancy because of divorce. The only important person in his life, until he met me, was his stepfather. I suppose Jock and I recognized each other's mutual hurts. He was very, very hard when I first knew him, but when he fell in love with me, his defences cracked like a shell.

'I met him at around the time I left home, which was also when I realized that I was tough enough to survive my parents' eternal battle. At sixteen I suddenly decided I simply didn't care about their fights any more. I just closed them off. Instead of feeling any pain over them, I became angry and forceful.'

Kate moved out of her mother's home and into her father's house for a year. Then she and Jock, together with five others, worked very hard at building up the home where they now live. They seem to find each other an emotional security that neither one has managed to get from anywhere else. And from rocky beginnings, they have both turned into mature young adults with feet firmly on the ground.

'If my parents could have given me the same reasons for their arguments and their separation; if, instead of bitching about each other, they could have seemed to back each other up, it would have been so much less hurtful.' That's Kate's view.

IT'S ALL MY FAULT

I have already mentioned that one of the classic reactions to the parents' separation is for the children to take the blame and the guilt for the break-up on themselves. This applies to children big and small.

'Max's stepfather and I split up when Max, who was then eleven, was away at his grandmother's,' says Dinah, Max's mother. 'I told him wnat had happened on the day he got back. That night he came down into the kitchen at midnight, very troubled and unable to sleep. "It's all my fault, isn't it Mum?"

he said. "If I hadn't gone away, none of this would have happened." Poor little boy.

'He's very wary now of any new relationships I make. And, interestingly, this drew him closer to his own father, who was particularly helpful at this time. I was thankful that Max was supported by him because I felt so bad that it was hard for me to do the supporting. Because Max was helped, I think I was too, indirectly.'

It *is* possible for parents to support each other during their divorce. Don't run each other down in front of the children, do back up the other partner's style of discipline, and do make it clear, if you can, that your principles of child-rearing are the same as your partner's even if your lifestyles are not. Such agreement is the ideal. But ideals may be out of reach and a more realistic aim would be maximum co-operation, however imperfect it may be in practice.

DISCIPLINE

A child needs a great deal of guidance, teaching and discipline between the ages of nine and thirteen. Just as child psychologists emphasize the importance of parents following through their teachings with the right example (if you tell Rosa not to eat chocolate, you mustn't either), they also emphasize the importance of parents backing each other up in their teachings.

D. W. Winnicott, a noted authority on children, says in his book *The Child, the Family and the outside world* (Penguin):

Father is needed to give mother moral support, to be the backing for her authority, to be the human being who stands for the law and order which mother plants in the life of the child. He does not have to be there all the time to do this, but he has to turn up often enough for the child to feel that he is real and alive. Much of the arranging of a child's life must be done by mother, and children like to feel that mother can manage the home when father is not actually in. Indeed, every woman has to be able to speak and act with authority; but if she has to be the whole thing, and has to provide the whole of the strong or strict element in her children's lives as well as the love, she carries a big burden indeed. Besides, it is much easier for the children to be able to have two parents; one parent can be felt to remain loving while the other is being hated, and this in itself has a stabilizing influence. Sometimes you see a child hitting or kicking his mother, and you feel that if her husband were backing her up, the child would probably want to kick him, and very likely would not try it on at all. Every now and again the child is going to hate someone, and if father is not there to tell him where to get off, he will hate his mother, and this will make him confused, because it is his mother that he loves most fundamentally.

Perhaps some of Winnicott's ideas about the roles of the male and female are old-fashioned, but there is a lot of basic good sense in what he describes. He is obviously describing the home where the parents are living together. And just as obviously, you don't get that kind of back-up when *he* has run off with the *au pair* girl or *she* has moved into the local commune. But even though there won't be any physical support, it is still possible to achieve a kind of mental solidarity with your ex-opposite number over child discipline.

I'm not suggesting the parent should get into the 'wait till your father hears about this' syndrome. That would be a mistake. But if, every so often, it were possible to compare notes about issues such as 'Is he allowed sweets at your place?' 'Are you having problems getting him to eat and, if so, how are you tackling it?' 'He seems to have developed a sudden interest in sex, what explanations are you giving him?', this would give common ground to work on and less scope for Bobby to play one of you off against the other.

As a lone parent you are going to be a lot more self-confident if you know that Bobby will get exactly the same kind of firm line over eating his baked beans at his father's house as he does when he is at home with his mother. And if Bobby begins to call you and everyone else filthy names, you are more likely to stick to your guns in dealing with him if you are convinced that you have got your spouse's back-up over it. How do you manage this? You use that magic instrument, the telephone, even if you have to go to a public call box.

I am not suggesting, of course, that you can't move a step without first getting the OK from your ex-spouse, but I do think that back-up between parents over subjects of childish controversy is a good idea for all concerned.

This kind of communication after divorce is the ideal. Of course, many people going through divorce will be so busy brandishing the meat axe every time they come within spitting distance of their spouse, that the possibility of such conversations seems mere wishful thinking. But if you only use these suggestions as a goal to work towards, you will be making a start. I firmly believe that we are able to change our behaviour, even if we can't change our basic personalities.

HOW CHILDREN COPE

In a recent American study by researchers Kelly and Wallerstein (1974), sixty families, which included children of all age groups, were observed and helped during divorce. The families were middle-class and white, and all lived in an urban district.

Striking differences were noticed in the behaviour of the seven- to eight-year-olds and nine- to ten-year-olds. Perhaps the most poignant of all was the reaction of pervasive sadness shown in the younger group. Unlike pre-school-age children in the study, who were able to explain away much of the divorce distress by creating fantasies and using denial, the seven- and eight-year-olds were too old to pretend. They were aware of their suffering but did not know how to relieve it. Since they were unable to analyse their feelings, as the older children could, they appeared immobilized. Most of them were worried about what would happen to them in the future, even going so far as to worry about whether there would be a home for them. Boys as well as girls did a lot of crying. And the feelings of insecurity showed clearly when they played and also in their constant demands for new clothes or toys. They felt particularly rejected by the departed parent, yet were unable to show anger against their parents.

In contrast, the nine to ten age group worked hard to master the conflicting feelings they were experiencing. They used denial, avoidance, courage, and activity to master their emotions as well as seeking support from others. Unlike the younger group, they did feel shame about the divorce and, as a result, frequently became very angry with their parents. They also felt lonely, partly because they could not see so much of one parent and partly because they felt the parent they lived with was too preoccupied with his or her own problems to concentrate on the emotional problems of the children. Fifty per cent of this age group found their progress at school had slackened off, and they did not see their friends so often, but a year later, most of them had returned to normal in these areas.

In the younger age group, on the other hand, only half improved on or maintained their earlier achievements after a year. The other 50 per cent either remained just as distressed and depressed or, in a few cases, became worse. The implications of these findings seem to be that seven or eight is just about the worst age for children to see their parents divorce. Children of pre-school age (three to five) also experienced emotions of shock, anger and depression, but most of them were able to regain their 'cool' within two or three months.

This survey also states emphatically that the better adjusted the child is before divorce, the more easily he is likely to come through it.

TEENAGERS

All emotionally healthy adolescents, be they products of divorce or a strong marriage, share one goal in common; how to achieve independence from their parents.

The 'teenage syndrome' is well-known. A previously well-behaved, well-adjusted, pleasant, and helpful young person turns, overnight it seems, into a moody, aggressive, rude, and defiant young man or woman. The change in mood, precipitated by the sudden fluctuations in hormone levels as a result of puberty, also heralds the struggle to break away from the people who, for the past twelve years or so, have been the main love objects of their life – their parents. Part of growing up demands a switch of allegiance from parents to a friend of their own age group. By switching their love, they can establish that they are now independent human beings in their own right. The vulnerable single parent, quick to blame the children's dramatic mood changes on divorce, can be reassured therefore that these difficult teenagers are probably much the same as anyone else's difficult teenagers. The effects of divorce added on to this process can over-burden young people and in many cases accelerates their growth towards independence.

The Wallerstein and Kelly study included twenty-one children over the age of thirteen who demonstrated surprisingly similar reactions to divorce. Each one of them found it a painful event, felt betrayed and angry, and had a sensation of loss. But they did *not* feel responsible for the marriage break-up; having reached a certain level of maturity, they were quite able to see that the break-up was between their parents and nothing to do with them.

All the teenagers used distancing and withdrawal as their methods of protection against emotional pain. They spent more time outside their homes, seeing more friends and making sure that they kept constantly busy. Later on, almost all the children were able to be emotionally supportive to their parents.

In another American study of teenagers and divorce, carried out by David Reinhard (1978), the young people who took part actually agreed that after they had emerged from the initial shock, they had a more mature and realistic view of their parents. They also saw themselves becoming more self-reliant.

There were, however, three teenagers in the Wallerstein and Kelly study who experienced a very adverse reaction. But, interestingly, each one of these seemed to be directly related to the parents' over-depressed reactions.

A thirteen-year-old boy, whose mother suffered from a severe hysterical illness and who had a history of suicide attempts, became far too protective of her, jealous of her dates, sleepless when she was out, and fearful that she would die of cancer. A year later, his reactions had intensified and he showed no signs of the normal teenage need to break away from his mother.

A thirteen-year-old girl had an intense relationship with her father although he had only communicated with his wife by notes for years. When the wife divorced him, the family did not see him again, although he paid them regular maintenance.

The daughter was particularly struck by his loss, became very depressed and continually worried about him. She lost her friends, played with dolls and much younger children, and slept with her mother. It took her two years to return to a more usual adolescent pattern of behaviour, and this coincided with her mother's re-marriage.

A third teenager, a fourteen-year-old girl, began having sexual adventures when she discovered her father was having an affair. She had fantasies about his sexual activities, threw rocks at his mistress' window, and started sleeping around. Her mother became depressed and took young lovers into the house, whereupon her daughter stepped up the promiscuity, drinking and taking drugs. A year later, nothing had changed.

Possibly these children might have been disturbed even if the marriages had lasted, since the family background of each one also seemed disturbed. These were the extreme reactions.

But even amongst those teenagers who had ended up by being helpful and supportive, there had been several problems along the way. Suddenly faced with a lack of parental restraint at a time when they needed some rules and regulations to kick against, they reacted by becoming aggressive and anti-social. The fact that their parents were no longer available to give them guidelines on sexual behaviour and outbursts of rudeness was confusing.

CONCLUSION

It does not help the teenager, struggling to sort out his confused feelings, to find that his parents themselves seem to have reverted to a state of adolescence. The young people who either benefited or were not hurt in the long run by divorce were those who were able to distance themselves from it right at the beginning. But in order to do this, they needed parents who could understand what their children were doing and why, and who did not try to prevent them from behaving in this way.

There have been no English equivalents of the Kelly and Wallerstein study detailed here, so we have no way of knowing if these American findings are pertinent to English children and adolescents. It is probably fair to assume that the basic points which emerge from the study are relevant; that the better the parents handle their relationship and eventually their divorce, the better adjusted their children of any age group are likely to be; that the older the children are, the more methods they are likely to dream up in order to cope with the initial shock; and that the more the parents can back each other up on issues of childcare, even if this involves a monthly telephone conference, the better it will be for their offspring. Divorce is *not* just a temporary crisis – it is a long-term situation.

TWO CASE HISTORIES

The following two case histories demonstrate something I have noticed during my personal interviews for this book, although I don't know of any research to act as supporting evidence. Namely, that children of divorce often marry young themselves – perhaps in an attempt to re-create the family life they felt was cut off from them as youngsters, perhaps as a method of escaping from what has become an uncomfortable home background.

Caroline

Caroline's parents divorced when she was fourteen. They had married very young and had grown apart from one another. Her father remarried immediately and within a year his new wife had produced a half-sister for Caroline.

Caroline lived with her mother, a very young and attractive woman who looks more like Caroline's sister than her mother. She occasionally stayed with her father and his new family, and got on amicably with them all, but nevertheless felt detached from them.

Her mother tentatively started dating at around the same time that Caroline did.

'That was quite fun,' says Caroline, 'but I did feel I was out of place in my own home then. There were times when it was obviously inconvenient for Mum to have a hulking great daughter around. By the time I was fifteen, I was going out practically every night.

'I think that if someone had encouraged me to stay on at

school then, I'd have done rather better there. But it didn't occur to either of my parents to do so. They were busy at that time with their own lives. By the time I reached sixteen I was in a hurry. I needed to have my *own* life. I left school and found a well-paid job as a secretary after a short training, then very rapidly fell in love.

'He certainly wasn't my first boyfriend but he was the first one I've ever taken seriously. He's very suitable husband material. We've been living together for two years [Caroline is now nineteen] and we've set the wedding date. I know I'm young to marry, especially since I've been with him since I was sixteen, but there doesn't seem much point in doing anything else. He's a nice man, good looking, earns a lot, is terribly suitable. I can't think of any reason not to marry him.'

What comes through from Caroline's conversation is an impression of aimlessness. She has grown up fast and now that she is there, she doesn't quite know what to do with being an adult.

Peter

Peter's parents divorced when he was thirteen and his mother remarried three years later. He didn't see his father again until he was thirty-five. He and his stepfather both tried hard to get on with each other.

'We succeeded quite well,' says Peter (now aged forty). 'I liked him a lot but he simply wasn't my real father. I was a very confused teenager, constantly wanting to be more adult than I actually was.

'I can remember, when I was thirteen, insisting that I acted as a kind of tourist guide for some young cousins who were staying with us (my mother was the manageress of a coastal hotel). Yet when I actually took them out somewhere, I spent most of the time blasting the unfortunate children with my new water pistol. I was really thirteen going on ten.

'I must have been daft becuse at sixteen I signed away the next three years of my life by joining the regular army. It was a manly sort of thing to do and it gave me the reassurance of knowing that for the next three years I would be provided with a roof over my head that wasn't my mother's. I came out at nineteen, looking visibly more adult but inside feeling terribly uncertain. I was longing for affection, I couldn't wait to get married. Since I was sixteen, getting married was the thing I had thought about most.

'I did marry the first girl who accepted me. It was disastrous. I was totally irresponsible. We had two children immediately, one within ten months of the other. Sylvia was pregnant when we married. I think I was scared she'd escape me otherwise. It was a continual struggle to survive. Nothing went right. I eventually had a nervous breakdown, lost my job and behaved appallingly. Not surprisingly, Sylvia and the kids left. I was back at square one, only now I was twenty-nine instead of nineteen and I don't think that emotionally I had learnt anything.

'Now, eleven years later, I have finally changed. That's really only because Julie, my second wife, has stuck to me through thick and thin. She's shown me that here is someone who isn't going to get up and leave when things go wrong. I'm eternally grateful to her and I do rely on her. She's like mother, father and lover rolled into one. I'm a much calmer, stronger person now; I actually have some self-confidence.'

4

What to Tell the Children

It is in those early weeks, when the wound of separation is raw and recent scenes are fresh and painful in the memory, that the hurt and confusion you are struggling through is mirrored by your children. 'Why are you crying Mummy?' 'Why doesn't Daddy live here any more?' 'What did Daddy do that was so bad?' The questions rain down on you, on top of the pain and hurt already inflicted, and it is hard not to lash back on reflex. But your children are unconscious casualties in this final sparring match, and so need nurturing and patience, not the unthinking cruelty of self-defence.

It is impossible to anticipate *all* those innocently provocative questions – 'Mummy, why doesn't Daddy like you any more?' – but you can certainly prepare yourself for a few. The following list contains what seem to be the most common questions. The answers have been gleaned from friends, child psychologists and children's psychiatric social workers. Of course, when you come to answer your children you will use your own words. My answers are just hints of how to go about it.

Q   Why are you getting divorced?
A   Because we haven't been getting along very well together. We've been unhappy for a long time. So now we think we might be happier if we live in separate homes.

Q Why did Daddy go away?

A (The answer may either be much as above or, if he has gone to live with another woman . . .) Because Daddy and Mummy haven't been very happy living together for quite a long time and now Daddy has met another woman with whom he thinks he *will* be happier. But Daddy still loves *you* very much and you will see him every week. (There's no point in beating around the bush. But it is important to reassure the children that Daddy still loves them, even if he doesn't love their mother any more.)

Q If you love Daddy so much, why did he leave?

A (This is a tricky question because it is a loaded one. It is important not to let the children make a connection with Daddy leaving Mummy even though she still loves him, and Daddy leaving the children, who also love him. It must be emphasized that, although the mother has been rejected, the children have not.) You can still love someone but find him very hard to live with. Both Daddy and I have been finding each other hard to live with. So we have decided to find different homes. But there will always be a home for you with me and you will have fun visiting Daddy often in his new flat.

Q But how can someone stop loving you?

A It's like forgetting someone very slowly. If you don't think about them very much, slowly you forget to love that person. Perhaps your love goes to a new person instead and that takes up the space of the old love. But Daddy is not going to forget or stop loving you. That's why he wants to see you at the weekends and in the holidays.

Q Will you still both be my mummy and daddy?

A We will always be your mummy and daddy. Nothing can ever, ever change that.

Q Will my brothers and sisters be with me?

A (Obviously depends on child custody arrangements. Either:) Yes, we are all going to carry on living together except for Daddy. (Or:) Your older brother is going to live with Daddy and you are going to stay here with me. But we will all meet up often. And sometimes you will stay with

Daddy and Brian and sometimes Brian will stay with you and me.

Q Why can't *I* go and live with Daddy?

A Because till you are older we think you will have a better time living with me. And, besides, I need you to keep me company. And Daddy needs Brian to keep him company.

Q I don't want you as my mummy any more. Why can't I live with my daddy?

A (This child is directing her anger about the divorce at the nearest available parent. Don't rise to the bait. And don't waiver in your confidence about the custody arrangements. The more she senses your feelings that the arrangements made are the *right* arrangements, the more she is going to feel secure. The angry child is also the one who is most likely to need a very big cuddle of reassurance at night.) I can understand that you feel angry about Daddy and I living apart. That's perfectly natural. And of course it won't be the same without Daddy. But it will be fun in a different way and we will be able to do different things. One of the things I thought we might do that was different would be to buy a dog. How do you feel about that? (For children over five years old, a dog is a sensible new project as it is something for them to direct their confused emotions towards, something to take their minds off their parents' problems, and a manifestation of the good part of your new life. It should not be offered in any way which makes it seem like a bribe, but simply as one of the several new schemes that this altered family unit is exploring.)

Q I don't want to live with you, Mummy. I want to go and live with my dad.

A (One of the main things resented by any child is the feeling of helplessness often experienced through *being* a child and therefore having no real control over life. The absent parent often seems more glamorous and attractive than the mundane old parent the child lives with. This combination of feelings makes children particularly sensitive to being thwarted and therefore they need to assert their independence. The more you can alleviate the feeling of helplessness, the better they will feel about their self-value. If they know that, they will feel less helpless and trapped.) You will be able to spend loads of time with Dad. You can get on the phone any time you want to speak to him. And as soon as you are old enough, you can ride your bicycle round to his place whenever you feel like it. (Recent French and American studies amongst divorced children have shown that the children with the most flexible access arrangements tend to be able to adjust best to divorce. Being able to ride a bike round to the other parent's house is specifically advocated in the American survey.)

Q I still want to go and live with my dad. Why can't I?

A (There comes a stage where the children will have to get used to the idea that, while everything possible will be arranged to keep them happy, they have *got* to accept that the decision for them to remain with their mother has been made by people more experienced than they are – who, when you get down to the nitty-gritty, know better. If they do not like it, gently but firmly make it clear that their feelings are unfortunate but that they will have to put up with and make the best of the present arrangements.) We have both decided it is better for you to remain with *me*, though you can see Daddy often. (Be prepared to say this politely but firmly several times over the next few weeks until they get used to it. It is important for the parent with custody to keep an open mind about access arrangements, however. If over a period of, say, a year, the child remains unhappy and becomes increasingly depressed, you may well have made the wrong decision and it would therefore be wise to change it. But it won't help things to be wishy-washy about the decision at the start of the separation.)

Q Why do you keep asking if I'm OK? I don't want to talk about you and Daddy any more.

A (Some children find it very difficult to discuss their feelings with a parent, simply because the conversation will be highly charged emotionally, especially if the children have seen many arguments and fights between the mother and father. It does not mean that there isn't a turmoil going on underneath their silence. If you have good reason to believe a child is very upset but is bottling it up, this is one of the occasions where it might be sensible to take her to a children's counsellor (See Chapter 2, page 9). It could be that she will find it easier to talk to a stranger than to emotive parents.) I'm sorry darling. I don't want to upset you. But I care about you and if you're feeling bad, I'd like to help get you to feel better. Perhaps you would feel more comfortable talking to a children's doctor without either of us there to listen. (If the answer is 'No', she doesn't want to talk to anyone at all, don't push it. She is entitled to the privacy of her thoughts, and may simply be trying to avoid something that causes her pain. One way of getting her to unburden herself a little is to talk about her other friends. If any of their parents are divorced, ask how the friend feels. Quite apart from giving her the opportunity to drop a few clues about her own feelings, it is a good idea to talk about what divorce entails to make sure she doesn't acquire any false preconceptions.)

Q Mummy, why doesn't Daddy like you any more?
A Because he's feeling very angry with me at the moment for wanting to divorce. I hope he'll like me better later on when he's got used to the idea.

Q Daddy says you've done something bad to him. What is it?
A I think he means that the bad thing was wanting to divorce. He feels badly about that right now.

Q Mummy, you say you love Daddy even though you want to divorce. Does that mean that it's Daddy's fault you are divorcing?
A No, it's never just one person's fault. And you can love someone as well as dislike them. Look at you. Sometimes you love me, sometimes you hate me when you get mad at me. Well, I'm the same. But Daddy and I were finding it hard to live together happily so we decided to change things. But there will always be a home for you with either of us. So you've always got both your parents to rely on, even if they are living in two different places.

Q Which one of you will look after me?
A It will be mostly me. I shall do all the looking after here, just

like I always have – the cooking, getting your clothes ready, taking you to school. And on the days when you're with Daddy, he will cook for you and look after you. (If Daddy hasn't done much in the way of housework previously, reassure her that he knows how.) Daddy *can* cook you know, he used to prepare terrific meals before we married.

Q What shall I tell my friends?
A Just tell them that your parents are getting divorced and that you will be living with your Mummy. If they want to know more, they'll ask you.

Q Mummy, you won't ever love anyone again like you did Daddy, will you?
A I won't ever love anyone in the same way as Daddy because you can only love Daddy like Daddy. But I might love someone else very much too. (Don't let yourself be emotionally blackmailed into saying things you don't mean and might regret later.)

Q Mummy, when are you going to get married again, to Daddy?
A (This may be confused thinking on the part of the children, but it is more likely to be wishful thinking. Simply explain gently but firmly for the hundredth time that you and Daddy are no longer living together, that you will not be getting married again to each other, that from now on you and he are leading separate lives. It can be hard to be firm about this when you have wistful youngsters badly wanting you to get back together again. But you will only be doing them a disservice if you give them false hopes with vague hints of a reunion. It is better that they face the truth.

Q Mummy, why does Granny say that Daddy is a no-good?
A (Make mental note to get very tough with Granny.) She doesn't really mean that Daddy's a no-good. What she means is that she's angry with him because of the divorce. She thinks it's all his fault. It isn't. But when Granny gets an idea into her head, it's sometimes very hard to change it. By calling him a no-good, she's really telling us that she's very cross.

Q Mummy, why don't you like Daddy any more?

A (Be truthful about your reasons while resisting the temptation to reel off a long list of Daddy's faults.) I need someone who is going to be able to help me more with my family and will do his share of the work in the house. Your Daddy has lots of other nice things going for him, but not those. And those things happen to be important to me.

Q Why were you so nasty to Daddy? If you'd been nicer he would have stayed with us.

A I was nasty because I was unhappy with Daddy. And when a person is unhappy they often behave badly. I wasn't the only one who was nasty, you know. Daddy was pretty unpleasant too. (This child has obviously worked out from the rows she has overheard that it is Mummy who has driven her father away. This may be true but she still needs some sort of an explanation.)

Q Are you going to get married again?

A (Obviously depends on what your plans are. If you have no immediate plans, it's best to say:) Not at the moment, darling, but I probably will one day. (Resist the temptation to swear never again. Because if you do go ahead and remarry later on, your children may remember this and find it harder to adapt to a new husband. On the other hand, if you are contemplating remarriage, and soon, but haven't yet told your children, introduce the possibility gradually. It's too much to expect them to adapt to an instant change in daddys.) I might marry my friend Michael one day. But I'm not really sure at the moment. I certainly hope I *will* get married again one day.

Q Did Daddy leave because of Michael?

A (Even if Daddy *did* leave because of Michael, it's better not to pin the responsibility for the divorce on the possible new stepfather's shoulders at this emotional stage of the separation.) Daddy and I had been getting along badly for a long time. Michael happened to come along at a particularly bad time and made me realize I would be much happier with him.

Q It's all my fault that Daddy went away, isn't it?

A No, it's not. It has absolutely nothing to do with you, or with anything you've done. The reason Daddy has gone away is because he was unhappy with me, not with you. He loves you very much indeed and will be seeing you as much as he possibly can. (It is vital to dispel any fears or notions children may have that something they have done is responsible for the marriage break-up. It is very common for a child to think this, and unless the idea is removed, it can result in some very depressed and unhappy behaviour.)

Q Now that Daddy's gone, does that mean I'm an orphan?

A Definitely not. An orphan is a child whose parents have both died. Your parents are very much alive and kicking and concerned about your welfare.

Q Now that I haven't got a daddy, does that mean I'm a bastard?

A No, dear. You are only a bastard if your Mummy and Daddy have never been married. You have got a daddy who was married to your mummy. It's just that he doesn't live with us any more.

Q Mummy, was it your fault that Daddy found a new girlfriend?

A It was nobody's fault. Daddy had stopped loving me and obviously needed some other lady to love, so he found his new friend.

Q Mummy, when will you find a new daddy for me?

A (It is important to children that everything in their life should conform. It is quite possible that you will find yourself pressurized by your child to make everything regular at home, by providing her with a permanent living-in dad, even though he is not the original one. This might be the time to make a mental note to ensure that she gets more male company, either in the form of more access to her father, or with her uncles, or simply with old friends who happen to be male. But don't let yourself get pushed into marrying someone simply because he seems a suitable stepfather. He also needs to be a suitable husband.) It's not so easy to find good new husbands. They are rather special people. But I'm keeping an eye open.

Q When is Michael going to leave? I don't like him. (Child asks about Mummy's boyfriend who is now living with them and who shortly intends to marry Mummy.)

A I'm sorry you don't like him. I expect you are jealous of his being Mummy's friend as well as you being Mummy's friend. But I'm afraid you will have to get used to living with Michael because he's going to be around for a long time. He loves me which is very nice for me. *You* have two people to love you, a mummy and a daddy. Well, I would like two people to love me as well, you and Michael. (It's not a good idea to thrust the possibility of your remarriage down your children's throat before they have had time to get used to your new partner. At the same time, they must gently but firmly be made to understand that *you* like him even though they don't. I believe in letting your children know when somebody loves you, even if they are jealous and resentful, because someone else's love and affection enhances a personal value about you that may well have been thrown out of the window by your previous partner during the marriage break-up. It is important that the children should have their feelings that you are a valuable person reinforced, even if the process does bring conflicting jealousies. It is easy for a child to feel emotionally responsible for the parent 'left behind', and this can be a heavy burden for a young person. You are effectively letting them off that hook if they can see that you are self-confident in yourself and valued by someone else.)

Q Are you going to marry Michael?

A (I repeat, this is *not* the time to say 'yes'. Your children need time to get used to a confusing change of male figures in their lives.) I may do, darling. I'm not quite sure at the moment. But I'm certainly enjoying living with him. If things keep on as well as they have done so far, it will be very nice to marry. But I'm not in any hurry at the moment.

Q Will Daddy die now that he's away from us?

A No, of course not, darling. He'll carry on working at his job and doing the same sort of things in his new home that he used to do here. He will be all right. He can take care of himself, you know. He's a big, grown-up man. He certainly won't die.

Q Why won't you buy me new toys any more?

A Because now that Daddy isn't living with us we don't have nearly so much money. What we do have has to be spent on important things like food and keeping warm, and on paying for our home. I wish we had a little extra to spend on playthings but unfortunately we don't. But we'll try and make some toys so that you've got something new to play with. (Make a mental note to enrol the child at the local library (free) if she is old enough to enjoy books and to investigate, through the library, the possibility of locating a toy library. There are a few scattered throughout England.)

Q Did Daddy leave because I didn't love him enough?

A (Another typical example of how children think it is *their* fault that Daddy left home. They have probably associated his departure with the last time they got the sulks and behaved badly, or with some small slight on their part.) Daddy's leaving has nothing to do with you at all. He didn't go because of anything you said or did or even thought. He left because he and *I* could not agree. Daddy loves you very much.

Q How should I explain your divorce to my friends?

A The best thing is to tell them what we have told you. Explain that your mummy and daddy are getting a divorce because they found it difficult to live together happily any more, therefore they have decided to live in two separate homes. So, from now on, you are going to have two homes. You'll probably find that some of your friends' parents are divorced as well.

Q Should I do the same with my relations?

A Yes, but be prepared for some of them to be very surprised at the news. Some people may be upset about it. I'm warning you about them so that *they* don't surprise and upset *you*.

Q Mummy, do you hate Daddy's new girlfriend?

A I don't like her very much because I'm angry with her for taking Daddy away. But I don't hate her. I expect I'll get used to her eventually, even though that's hard to imagine right now. (This tells the truth, yet shows that adults are capable of changing their feelings in the same way that children are.)

The questions and answers here have been worded for families where it is Dad who has left home. They will, of course, be very similar when it is Mum who has moved out.

The essence of these explanations lies in expressing yourself straightforwardly, in reassuring the children, and in not overdoing the bitter feelings you almost certainly have towards your spouse.

It is important to understand that children go through a long period of trying to work out these major changes in their lives, why they happened and what these circumstances have to do with them. It is as natural for the children to need to talk about their feelings in order to sort them out as it is for you to do so. And if any of you are bottling up these feelings, too unhappy to make a murmur, both parent and children should try to realize that it is a good idea to get them out somehow. Even if it's hard for you, the bereft parent, to find someone to talk the break-up over with, at least you should have the satisfaction of knowing you can provide a platform for discussion for your children.

The explanations here have been geared for a young child, between three and five years old. Naturally, you will have to interpret them on a level to suit your own offspring.

There are many divorce situations that these questions and answers don't cover – for example, the deserted parent who heartily hates the departed one and honestly feels that it's better never to see him again, or the departed parent who has managed to brutalize the family previously. The questions and answers also assume that the parent left behind is emotionally capable of answering the children's questions in the first place, when this is of course not necessarily the case.

But however explosive and traumatic the marriage break-up has been, the children's situation in divorce remains much the same whatever the circumstances. In later years, even though this is slight consolation during the actual crisis, those feelings will simmer down and you will wish you had behaved more wisely at the time. The only cases where it would be wiser to avoid 'being fair' to the departed parent are in cases of physical cruelty where you and the children have been in actual bodily danger. In those cases it is better to explain (if indeed it needs explanation) that Daddy/Mummy was sadly a difficult and dangerous man/woman and you are safer living without him/her. But it is *only* in these cases that an explanation of that sort is wise.

Then there are the cases where the parent departing has been so difficult to live with that he seems dangerously unbalanced to the point of insanity?

Some people behave worse with one partner than with another, so it is possible that the two of you will both become considerably more normal on leaving each other, a fact which should reassure you about the children's contact with their other parent. It is probably best to explain to them that together you and Dad behave badly but that apart you are both likely to be nicer people.

Jane and Ian sent each other to extremes of anger in their marital battles, yet separately they were charming and well-balanced people. Jane eventually met another man who lived life at a less volatile pace. His low-key emotions seemed like a haven to a storm-tossed refugee and she left Ian to set up home with her lover.

On his own, Ian went through the divorce syndrome of sorrow, grief, anger, and bitterness, but emerged to meet a woman who possessed the same qualities as himself, someone who was able to thrive on the arguments that make up a stimulating side of Ian's life. Three years later they are quarrelling, but amicably and without a thought of anything other than remaining married to each other. Both Jane and Ian have been able to become happier and better balanced people with new partners.

Their two children had hated the battles between their parents and had behaved in quite a disturbed way during this time. Once they were able to feel for themselves that their parents were happier though apart, the children also settled down.

They were quick to grasp that adults show a variety of behaviour, all of which is normal to those particular individuals. They had no difficulty in accepting the different standards in their two homes, and settled into each amicably. Their schoolwork improved and they made friends. Their parents made a point of living near each other and the children spent an equal amount of time at each home. Perhaps the most valuable result of the separation was that, after a couple of years, even Jane and Ian got on better together.

If the departed one seems insane (such as the pathologically jealous type, the schizophrenic, the hard-line alcoholic or drug addict, the severely depressed, the person with acute paranoia) to the extent where it is feared he may show extreme violence, this of course is considerably beyond the marital 'insanity' just described. This *would* be a case where you and your family need protection and it should be explained to the children in terms of 'illness'. As with any kind of illness though, these kinds of symptoms can improve and it is important not to lose sight of that possibility. It is, however, a situation where, for everyone's safety, outside authorities should be notified. It may be in your and your children's interests, when the custody of the children comes to be decided, that people like your GP and your local social worker have it formally on record that your spouse has created anti-social problems in the past. But, I hasten to add, some of the maddest husbands and wives have simultaneously managed to be excellent parents, a fact which should be kept firmly in perspective.

George Denham is fifty-five and has been divorced from his wife for nine years. He is obsessive, depressed and often paronoiac. On these grounds, his wife was easily able to obtain total custody and care and control of their three children, as her husband's 'eccentricities' were well-known to the local authorities. (One of his obsessions was to write letters of complaint to the social work department.)

Unfortunately, Mrs Denham is not a particularly good influence on the children because she drinks a great deal and allows her seventeen-year-old son to do likewise. There are constant drunken parties going on in their home. The eldest daughter got away from the disruption these cause by marrying and leaving the district. The youngest daughter, aged fourteen, would often walk the streets at night rather than go home. She was also very poorly clothed, as her mother never had enough money to buy anything decent.

Mr Denham, denied any access at all to his children, had managed to keep up contact with his youngest daughter by subterfuge and seems to have a good caring relationship with her. He was very distressed when he found her out on the street one night. He took her straight to his lodgings, made sure she had a room of her own, a decent diet and some new clothes. She in turn felt happier for being looked after, and wanted to stay with him.

Her mother, however, protested strongly to the local social worker and, with no difficulty at all, had the girl placed back under her roof. But she did not change her way of life, although she had promised to.

George Denham is now fighting an almost impossible battle to convince the local probation officer that he should have care and control of his daughter. Unfortunately, his reputation as an unbalanced husband makes this virtually impossible. The result? Impasse – and one very damaged teenage girl. Yet, in spite of his 'mad' record, he seems like a good caring parent, better fitted to house the daughter than his ex-wife.

I suspect that nearly every divorce case has at least an element of such bitter disagreement that it amounts to a type of insanity on the part of either parent. Couples often push each other to the edge of this kind of madness, while in many other ways they are perfectly sane and balanced human beings. Try to remember the sane and balanced bits *as well as* the mad bits when it comes to sorting out the desirability of a continued relationship between departed spouse and child.

Mary and Colin were temperamentally unsuited. At the start of their marriage they found their opposite characters to be stimulating. But once they had a family, Colin's obsession with efficiency began to seem oppressive to Mary, while Mary's easy-going attitudes nearly drove Colin to despair. Appalling rows ensued over such minor details as doing the ironing on the wrong day or throwing away flowers that weren't quite dead. The relationship, further aggravated by Colin's tensions at work and Mary's fatigue from coping with a young family, did not survive the strain.

The divorce found each trying to nail the other for unreasonable behaviour. Yet each one, when forced to be reasonable about the other by their lawyers, rediscovered the many engaging and 'sane' aspects of their personalities which had made the first years of the marriage very happy ones.

'It was about then that I understood the pointlessness of being enraged with Colin,' explains his ex-wife. 'I'd catch myself tearing my hair out in front of the kids and find they were looking at me in astonishment. They simply couldn't see what he had done that seemed so insane to me. I suddenly realized I must appear even more mad than he did.

'After that, I managed to accept that we simply had our differences and that we would be better off living apart. It meant I could explain the break-up more rationally to the kids, which I now realize was just as well. Colin, unfortunately, was not able to understand our mutually generated madness and carried on ranting and raving about me. It was lucky for the children that at least one of their parents was able to be nice about the other. It made them better balanced and happier about themselves.'

John and Christina's child, Anna, sadly never knew anything but her parents constantly harping at each other.

'I remember when I was sixteen,' says Anna, 'and my parents had already lived apart for ten years, suddenly blocking myself off from my mother. After all that time she was still going on about how weak-minded my father was and how his defects had ruined her life. Only the day before, I'd heard my father saying, for the millionth time, how mad my mother was and how it was impossible to rely on her for anything.

'I hated them for it. I remember feeling quite cold and thinking, from now on I'm not going to listen to either of them. They're incapable of controlling their own lives, so from now on they're not controlling mine.

'My behaviour changed from that time onward. I stopped being patient and tactful with my mother and told her what I really thought. She threw me out and I went to live with my Dad and his girlfriend. That was a bit better but I felt badly in need of my own home. So when I met up with the first boy I ever really cared for, he and I squatted in an empty house which we lived in for the next three years.'

It was not perhaps the most sensible way of life for a sixteen-year-old who was taking her exams and trying to get to university. It is perhaps a tribute to Anna's precocious maturity that she slogged away at her school work and got a university acceptance in spite of everything. She puts down that maturity to having mentally endured her parents' marital battles for years. It is one advantage gained from the marital warfield, but Anna would be the first to agree that the disadvantages heartily outweigh the balance.

If there is some doubt about the departed parent's influence on the children, if you suspect that they really are being upset or unsettled, it is fair to give parent and children a chance to let things settle down first. Let them see each other a number of times before deciding against further access. You should not make a judgement on the basis of Johnny looking upset after just two visits.

Only if you are *absolutely sure* that the other parent is being truly harmful should you think about limiting that access. And I'm hesitant about writing even that because I know many bitter parents will seize on it as an excuse to use their children as pawns.

Seeing a parent immediately after separation *is* upsetting. It's probably normal for the children to feel terrible. The real question arises when, after a decent number of visits, the children seem worse rather than better. Then and only then is it time to re-think the access. How long is a decent number of visits? It's impossible to generalize. *You* know your children best. Just try and remember, it's *their* upset you're gauging, not *yours*.

Younger children naturally will need this kind of decision made for them. Older children should have their opinions sought and taken into account. Less access for a few months might help everyone cool down and give the parent who has left home breathing space, time in which to get his new life more organized. Once he is more settled, he is likely to be more relaxed with the family.

Access can always be varied. There is no reason why it shouldn't be flexible. It could be resumed again regularly after three or six months if that seems desirable.

Should the children themselves tell you they don't want to see their father or mother again, bear in mind the following story.

Matthew, Jimmy and Carole were aged between fifteen and eleven when their father left their mother for a much younger woman. Seeing their mother depressed and unhappy, the children found it impossible to understand or forgive him and unanimously refused to visit him.

Today, seven years later they are young adults. Their father has remarried and they have a half-brother they've never seen. Now the eldest son regrets that he has had no contact. He would like to be friends again but as he says, 'It's very hard to make that first move when I've rejected him all these years. I just don't think I can do it.' His might have been a good case for insisting right at the beginning that he and his brother and sister should visit even if only very occasionally.

Perhaps the best thing I can say is, play it by ear. Be sensitive to your children's emotional welfare and mentally stamp on any inclination to use their access as a weapon.

What if the departed partner very obviously doesn't care if he/she never has any contact with the child again, has never cared for the child and is never likely to change? What is the least hurtful way of dealing with this?

Again, it probably won't need much in the way of explanation. A child of any age knows whether or not someone is interested in it and has therefore, sadly, probably already been through the same pangs of rejection and subsequent toughening up that you have experienced. Rather than asking questions you may find the child heaving sighs of relief at eventually getting rid of the uncaring parent.

Jenny and Michael were six and four when their father eventually moved out. They hardly seemed to notice his departure, although their mother, Liz, fell over herself to ensure they all kept in touch. As far as the children were concerned, their father was simply keeping to a pattern that had been there all their young lives, one of dissociation. They much preferred their new stepfather, who did take an interest in them and cared for them. When a friend of their mother's asked them if they were sad that their father had left, they seemed puzzled by the question. It hadn't occurred to them to mind; their father was not someone they had cared about strongly in the first place.

And what about the parents who are so depressed and grief-stricken that they simply cannot discuss any of the divorce with their child? If you can understand that your child does have a need for information and reassurance from someone, but if it simply can't be you who gives it, the best thing to do is to try to find someone who *can* talk to them to explain it for you.

Barbara's marriage broke up, quite unexpectedly, after twenty years of relatively happy life together. There was 'another woman' involved. The break-up coincided with the beginning of Barbara's menopause so she suffered deep depression, a loss of self-confidence and a sense of being devalued. She was quite incapable of talking about the break-up coherently with her children, and it was five years before she began to feel anything like normal. Her eldest son was seventeen at the time and was sensitive enough to understand and sympathize deeply with his mother and to fill in as a parent figure with the two youngest children, then aged nine and seven. He was the one who patiently gave the explanations over the months, he was the one who aranged access with his father.

Even now, none of the children from that first marriage has the slightest desire to visit their father's new home, to meet their father's second wife or even to meet their new little half brother, although they do take turns to spend every Sunday with their father on some outing. Of the four children of that first marriage it is the second, aged fifteen at the time of the break up, who seems to be the least well-adjusted member of the family at the moment. Perhaps it is because he was the only one who never somehow got a proper chance to talk things through, perhaps he just happened to be at a very emotional and impressionable phase in his life, or perhaps he would have been the least 'well-adjusted' child whether his parents' marriage had survived or not. It is almost impossible to sort out the true solution. But at present he does appear to be opting out of the mainstream of life.

The message therefore reads – talk about the divorce if you possibly can.

5

Where Can I Get Help?

Separation and divorce usually mean practical and physical, as well as emotional, upheaval. The financial facts invariably dictate that each divorcee enjoys a depleted standard of living, that juggling children and jobs becomes a necessity, that Britain's appalling lack of nursery care makes itself painfully felt, and that housing becomes an urgent problem. In addition, if your children are very young, it may mean giving up work to live on social security. You may have to struggle with the red tape of bureaucracy to obtain special grants. You can be penalized for having a normal sex life if you happen to be a woman who needs to live on social security.

To the bereaved parent with the responsibility of the children heavy on his or her hands, these problems often seem insurmountable. It is hard to know where to start. 'I remember being so depressed after my wife left us that I couldn't work out in the morning which clothes belonged to which child. They all looked like jumble. As for coping with a job, it took me two years to get back to my old employment,' said Mr R.M. of South London. He had three children aged two, six and eight at the time of separation.

In an attempt to sort out a little order from the chaos, I am listing the names and addresses of all the most useful organizations for giving practical help and support with such vital needs as jobs, housing and childcare.

DAY CARE FOR CHILDREN UNDER FIVE

A relative may be able to look after your baby, or perhaps you can afford to hire outside help. Often a carefully worded advertisement in a local paper will result in a 'granny', experienced in bringing up her own children and sympathetic towards yours. Most of these women are not registered child-minders, however, and you therefore employ them at your children's risk.

Otherwise the choice is between council or private day nurseries, or crèches provided by employers. Playgroups and nursery classes may be helpful if you have a part-time job.

DAY NURSERIES RUN BY LOCAL AUTHORITIES

These nurseries are staffed by trained nursery and medical nurses. They are often very over-subscribed, so get yourself on the waiting list immediately. Most councils give priority to single parents. If you are waiting for a nursery place *before* you get a job, you must find a job within two weeks or so of your child starting at the nursery. Most councils insist that you live or work within the local authority area and some insist that you are working for thirty hours a week, although others accept part-timers. Not all accept student parents. Cost usually depends on your income. Some councils impose a minimum charge. It is an advantage if your GP or social worker supports your application. Health visitors can also help with obtaining day nursery vacancies.

PRIVATE DAY NURSERIES

A list of these is available from your social services department of the local authority, whose number will be in the telephone directory. Private day nurseries are run on similar lines to council nurseries, except that they cost more and often have shorter hours. The average fee at the time of writing is £20–30 a week.

CHILD-MINDER

A child-minder is usually a housewife with children of her own who wants a job to fit in with her domestic arrangements. She will look after your child in her own home. In theory, she should be registered with the local authority but, in practice, she may not be. It is sensible to check on this.

It is difficult to tell how good a child-minder each individual is likely to be. But you can make some attempts to find out. Call on her beforehand. Have a good look at her home, and watch the other children in the household for a bit if you can. Are they happy or are they lying in cots with nothing to do? Find out what her programme is for the children each day. If you have any reason to think they are not being looked after properly, get in touch with the social services department.

A child-minder's hours can usually be aranged to correspond with your working day. The cost at the moment is around £15 a week. If you do not know of any child-minders, the social services department keeps a list of those registered with them. Sometimes, child-minders advertise in the local newspapers too.

EMPLOYERS' CRÈCHES

A few enlightened employers – hospitals, some unions and some industrial companies – provide crèches for employees' children. Sometimes universities and colleges of higher education do too. These crèches are generally supervised by trained staff and offer facilities similar to day nurseries. The advantages of having a crèche at work are tremendous, though. You can see your child during the day if you need to, and there is no problem about timing.

Factory and company crèches are not registered but the personnel manager of any particular company or the local employment exchange will be able to inform you if or where they exist.

The Royal College of Nursing, 1a Henrietta Place, London W1 (01-580 2646) will have information about hospital crèches. Or you can phone the secretary of your area health authority for information. A list of college crèches can be provided by the National Union of Students, 3 Endsleigh Street, London WC1 (01-387 1277) on receipt of a large SAE.

PRIVATE (PAID) HELP

1. You can find a nanny through a domestic employment agency (addresses of these agencies appear in the classified sections of magazines such as *The Lady* and *Nursery World*). You can also advertise for a nanny yourself in these magazines. Local papers are good places to advertise, too. Some training colleges for nursery nurses like their students to get some practical experience. So, if you apply to the colleges direct, you may be able to find a good, competent nanny for a less expensive wage. Nannies are generally very experienced trained children's nurses who live in.

2. Mother's helps are generally young, untrained women. They may, nevertheless, be caring and sympathetic towards children, and have a reliable sense of responsibility. They would probably be more reliable on a part-time basis rather than a full-time one, since someone so young would probably find the strain of caring for children too much to take on for eight hours a day. Mother's helps can also be found through the classified columns of *The Lady* and *Nursery World*, and local papers. School leavers may be interested in a job of this kind, too. If you contact the careers officer at your local secondary school towards the end of a term (the summer term is of course the time you are most likely to find a school leaver), he or she may be able to suggest several suitable candidates. A mother's help normally lives in.

3. You can arrange to employ an *au pair* through domestic employment agencies, or advertise for one in *The Times* or the *International Herald Tribune*. Although *au pairs* are a cheaper form of home help, they tend to be unsatisfactory unless you have a very part-time job because their hours are also part-time. Further hazards are that their English may be non-existent and their hours will be relatively short. They live in.

4. A local granny may provide daytime help similar to that given by a mother's help. Inquire or advertise in the

neighbourhood. Hours and wages depend on what you both find acceptable.

PLAYGROUPS

These would only be of use to part-time workers because they are part-time. A list of local groups will be available from the social services department or from the Citizens Advice Bureau.

NURSERY SCHOOLS AND NURSERY CLASSES

The purpose of nursery school or class is education through play rather than childcare. Hours vary from school to school. Some operate all day, some are for mornings or afternoons only. They cater for children aged between two and five. The nursery classes are usually attached to state primary schools. A list of schools and classes is available from the local education authority. It is best to apply as early as possible because there may be a waiting list, but priority is given to single parents. State nursery education is free, while private schools may cost anything from £20 to £30 a week. The Montessori schools throughout the country are of a specially high standard.

GINGERBREAD

Gingerbread is a nationally organized self-help association for one-parent families. Membership is open to anyone who shares its aims and objectives. At the time of writing, there are over 400 local groups in all parts of the country. The groups meet regularly and arrange social activities for parents and children, and practical help is given to members on a co-operative and collective basis.

Amongst the schemes at present run by Gingerbread is the Gingerbread House in Croydon, where local children from one-parent families are given after-school and holiday care in a large old house, looked after by full-time and part-time paid workers. The Gingerbread Holiday Scheme enables single parents to have holidays by exchanging or sharing their homes with others. In Liverpool there is a 'pop-in' centre where a local solicitor offers help and advice, babysitting is available, and childcare arrangements for holidays are also provided.

Gingerbread supplies a number of leaflets on such things as legal rights, housing, mortgages, and future income, plus advice to parents on a wide variety of problems. Its national headquarters is at 35 Wellington Street, London WC2 and help is given not only to Gingerbread members but to all lone parents.

NATIONAL COUNCIL FOR ONE PARENT FAMILIES

The National Council for One Parent Families, 255 Kentish Town Road, London NW5 2LX (01-267 1361) is the only national charity which deals exclusively and professionally with all problems faced by one-parent families. It advises individuals, the public and the Government on matters of family law, childcare, povery, welfare rights, housing, health, tax, employment, and emotional problems.

AFTER-SCHOOL AND HOLIDAY CARE FOR SCHOOL-AGE CHILDREN

Schools

A few primary and secondary schools remain open after school hours, usually making the playground available to children waiting to be collected. They may stay open until 6.30 and also remain open in the holidays. You can find out which schools do this by getting in touch with the local education authority.

Big city authorities such as the ILEA organize a variety of holiday schemes for children. Local authorities have various holiday schemes too, and there may be others run by voluntary organizations in your area. The local authority or the local library will usually have details of what is available.

Church of England Children's Society
This organization runs a variety of children's homes and childcare centres, and provides special help for single parents during and after school and in the holidays. These cheerful and welcoming homes are situated in England and Wales. For full details, write to Church of England Children's Society, Old Town Hall, Kennington Road, London SE11, or ring 01-735 2441. You don't have to be Church of England to qualify for help.

Housing Associations
A few housing associations also have special childcare facilities. Examples of such associations are Nina West Homes and New Swift, but for a full list get in touch with the housing Corporation, 149 Tottenham Court Road, London W1P 0BN.

Private Help
You could advertise for help on a part-time basis or a full-time basis to fit in with school hours and your job or commitments. Once again, a local gran or a young housewife may fill the bill very well.

JOBS

It is important to weigh up the value of the job and the cost of childcare while you are out at work. It may be that you would be financially better off on Supplementary Benefit with the advantage of being able to look after your children personally which, if they are young, is of great value.

Full-time Work
Naturally, the nearer your job is to your children's nursery or school, the better. You will need a fall-back arrangement, too,

in case the children are ill, so you should make sure you know who would be prepared to come in and look after them. One of the best places to work from the point of view of holidays is a school, as a teacher or a secretary, or on the domestic staff.

If you had a career before having children, or indeed are still continuing with it, you of course stand the best chance of earning well by pursuing your original training or talent. It is important to emphasize that if you can stick to work which is familiar, it will make life more comfortable. When you are coping with the trauma of divorce and the strain of being a single parent *and* breadwinner, it makes sense to do what comes most easily. It also means that you are more likely to get promotion and earn more.

If you are looking for a new job, though, it is certainly worth trying to find one where provision for childcare is made.

Part-time Work

One way of managing to work part-time and look after the children too is to take temporary jobs. If you are a secretary you can work as a 'temp', which means you are the one who decides what hours to accept. It means you can work in the term time and holidays to fit in with your children's schedule. You can claim Supplementary Benefits during the holidays when you are out of work. There are also a number of jobs that are seasonal, such as work on farms and holiday (tourist) jobs. Many small businesses need part-time workers too.

Freelance Work

This is the ideal kind of work to combine with bringing up children. The disadvantage is that your income may not be steady. Jobs such as journalism or market research, outwork or illustrating are just a few obvious ones that spring to mind. But if you don't have a particular training or a special talent, you could make use of your domestic talents to care for someone else's children, to do hairdressing for friends, or to become a cook supplying home-made food to stores or direct to other mothers.

Residential Work

A live-in job means you combine job, home and salary. It may seem the solution to many problems but one of the snags of living on top of the job is that it tends to surreptitiously take over your life. Most of the living-in jobs where your children will be accepted too will be of a domestic help/mother's help sort. One of the best ways to find a good job is by advertising yourself in *The Lady* or *Nursery World*, or by replying to some of the advertisements in these magazines. Local papers sometimes carry details of these jobs, and Gingerbread and the National Council for One Parent Families (see pages 63 and 64 for addresses) also have jobs registers.

Single Handed Ltd is a commercial agency set up to help single parents find residential jobs and to put single parents who want to share accommodation in touch with each other. Their address is 68 Lewes Road, Haywards Heath, Sussex (0444 54663).

Career Advice

Equal Opportunities: A Careers Guide by Ruth Miller (Penguin) lists every possible profession you can think of with detailed explanation of what it consists of, what training you would need and what prospects you might expect.

The Equal Opportunities Commission issues a booklet called *Fresh Start* which is a guide to re-training, aimed mainly at women who need to come back to a job after some years away from work. It is available free from the EOC, Overseas House, Quay Street, Manchester M3 3HN.

HOUSING

The first piece of advice is to hang on to your present accommodation if it is at all possible and find out what help you are entitled to and what your legal position is before making any moves. Detailed information on husbands' and wives' rights to the family home in the event of divorce is provided in *Women's Rights, A Practical Guide*, Anna Coote and Tess Gill (Penguin), so I am not going into similar detail here. The areas covered by the book are: what to do in the event of the family property being in the husband's name, in the wife's name, in joint names; how to safeguard a matrimonial right; how to claim a share of the family property during marriage; what share you may be entitled to; what legal arrangements are likely to be made to divide the property; what can be done legally if you have nowhere to live after divorce; what happens to rented property after divorce, whether it is private or council owned; what happens, if you have a joint tenancy, if the tenancy is in the husband's name or in the wife's.

If you can possibly stay on in your present family home, this is the best thing to do because it is familiar to your children, will be reassuring to you all and will be one less change to cope with.

If this is impossible, you must seek expert legal advice over your legal rights to maintenance and provision for housing. For property advice and information on rights, contact one of the housing aid organizations (see page 71).

Mortgage Repayments

If a partner suddenly has to cope with mortgage repayments single-handed, and also has to live on Social Security, Social Security will pay the interest on the mortgage, though not the capital repayments. If you get into arrears with mortgage repayments, you will have to contact the lending source (building society or local authority) and explain the situation. Most are sympathetic and will make arrangements for you to defer capital repayments until you have arranged your finances and maintenance. In some cases you may not have to pay for as long as a year. What you are effectively doing is extending the period of your loan – the arrears will be added on to the end of your repayment time.

If your financial situation is such that you will not be able to resume mortgage payments after a while, though, you will be forced to sell your house and give a lump sum to the building society to cover the remainder of the loan.

One way of coping with the extra sums needed to keep up your mortgage may be to take in a lodger. But check your position regarding tax before taking this step.

You may find that, if your spouse has the right to a lump sum from the proceeds of selling the house, the remaining money is not enough to put down on a cheaper property. In these circumstances, avoid selling the house if you possibly can. The Child Poverty Action Group (see page 72) may be able to offer you some help with your mortgage.

Finding a New Home
If you can afford to do so, it is sensible to buy a house. *Women's Rights* (see page 67) gives details on getting a mortgage. If you cannot afford to buy, there are alternatives. The first is to rent a home.

Private Renting. It has been extremely difficult to rent privately since the Rent Act of 1965 made many landlords sell off their property rather than rent it. The best ways to find a flat or house are to consult estate agents, read the small ads in local newspapers, and ask your friends. Invariably, the best way of all to find a rented flat is through personal contact.

Council Renting. You can find out how easy or difficult this may be by visiting the housing department of the local council (the address will be in the telephone book). Some areas, such as big cities, have long waiting lists for council accommodation, while other areas – for example, in Derby – have empty houses waiting for occupation.

Councils will normally only house families and old people. A single parent with children counts as a family. A pregnant woman doesn't, although the rules change if she is homeless. Even if the council has nothing for you immediately, it is worth putting your name down on their waiting list. And you have to see that your name is kept on a council list by re-applying at whatever intervals the local authority lays down.

If you are actually homeless (with children), the council has a duty to house you. The trouble is that you may find yourself put in sub-standard accommodation, or lodged for many months in a seedy private hotel.

Although, in theory, the council should eventually re-house you in reasonable accommodation, it is sometimes not possible because they don't have enough property. If, because of difficulties in housing, there is any likelihood that your children might actually be taken away from you, get in touch with Shelter or the Catholic Housing Aid Society (see page 71 for addresses). The National Council for Single Parents (see page 64) is used to fighting these battles too, so you can ask them for help.

Housing Associations. Housing associations provide a third form of housing. Here you invest a small premium in state-subsidized property and/or pay a reasonable rent (again, it is state-subsidized). In return, you become a member of one of a variety of housing associations. In some you gain a capital investment in the property as you continue to pay, and when you want to leave you will be able to get out of it at least what you put in. In others, you have the advantage of living in good accommodation at an extremely low rent. In others, you become part of a co-ownership scheme. This means that everyone in your group or block jointly owns the whole collection of properties and is not only responsible for individual accommodation but also for the administration of the properties as a whole. This last group of associations works on several levels, depending on the particular scheme, from families in individual apartments to groups of people living communally.

The National Council for One Parent Families will be able to advise on local schemes, while general advice can be sought from the National Federation of Housing Associations, 30–32 Southampton Street, London WC2 (01-240 2771). Some of the housing associations throughout the country are specially geared to single parents or give priority to single parents, and some have special childcare projects incorporated in them.

As with most types of housing, there are usually waiting lists. But this accommodation tends to become available rather faster than other types and it is worthwhile registering as soon as you think there may be a possibility of needing somewhere to live.

Licensed Squatting. As a last resort – and I emphasize this because squatting tends to involve hard work and privation – licensed squatting might provide you with short-life accommodation. The advantage of licensed squatting is that, if you have a family, you are likely to be re-housed eventually. Licensed squatting entails paying a minimal rent for the use of property that is due for demolition in a short time but is just about habitable. Many local councils let out this property on short leases and it is official, legal and legitimate. It is not to be confused with illegal squatting where homeless people break into empty property and start living there. Shelter will advise on the feasibility of licensed squatting in individual cases.

Housing Aid

Shelter, 157 Waterloo Road, London SE1 (01-633 9377) is a national campaign for the homeless. It has aid offices in England, Scotland and Wales and will supply a list of these on request. Shelter exists to help people with all kinds of housing problems, including those arising from family break-up. Once clients have come to them with a specific housing problem, they are taken on until the problem has been solved.

Catholic Housing Aid, 189a Old Brompton Road, London SW5 (01-373 4961/2) works in a similar way to Shelter. The London branch takes on individual cases and it will supply a list of the thirty local branches which do the same. It is open to people of all faiths.

Shac, 189a Old Brompton Road, London SW5 (01-373 7276) is a telephone advice organization dealing with the whole of the London area. Amongst their specialities is a house purchase department.

Both **Gingerbread** and the **National Council for One Parent Families** (see pages 63 and 64 for addresses) can help with housing registers and housing advice.

USEFUL READING

Rights, Guide for Homeowners, Jo Tunnard and Clare Whately; available by mail order from Shac, 189a Old Brompton Road, London SW5.

A Woman's Place: Family Break Up and Housing Rights, Maureen Leevers and Pat Thynne; also available from Shac.

EMOTIONAL AND PRACTICAL SUPPORT

Gingerbread (see page 63).

National Council for One Parent Families (see page 64).

Scottish Council for Single Parents, 44 Albany Street, Edinburgh EH1 3QR (031 556 3899) and 39 Hope Street, Glasgow G2 6AE (041 221 1681). Advice, information and referral. The council sorts out the appropriate services for single-parent families. It holds conferences and has a list of useful publications available by mail order.

Child Poverty Action Group, 1 Macklin Street, London WC2 (01-242 3225). Advice and help for low-income families on welfare benefits and other problems.

Families Need Fathers, 97c Shakespeare Walk, London N16 8TB (01-953 8932). This is a group of divorced men and women who fight for the rights of fathers when custody has been granted to the mother. They supply leaflets about their group.

Mothers Apart from their Children (MATCH), BM Problems, London WC1N 3XX (01-892 9949). A group of divorced or separated mothers who have chosen to let their ex-husbands have custody of their children. They provide a crisis counselling service, emotional support and a media service which aims at informing the public that the decision to live apart from the children can be a responsible and caring one.

National Children's Home, 85 Highbury Park, London N5 1UD (01-226 2033). As well as running many children's homes all over the country, NCH gives help to families, including financial and housing aid. It employs full-time social workers, and runs family centres incorporating twelve-hour day care with medical and educational facilities, and can help with accommodation often specially designed for one-parent families. They also run advice centres and playgroups.

National Federation of Clubs for the Divorced and Separated, 13 High Street, Little Shelford, Cambridge, CB2 5BS. This organization, which has over 100 branches in the UK, operates on both a social work and a counselling level, but the clubs are mainly social. There is regular members' newsletters, and help and advice with problems can be given.

National Federation of Solo Clubs, 8 Ruskin Chambers, 191 Corporation Street, Birmingham 4 (021 236 2879). This has 150 local branches which often advertise in the classified columns of local newspapers. The branches organize meetings, dancing, theatre parties, coach trips, outings and so on for lonely men and women and their children. They have a benevolent fund and can provide holiday help. They also supply a booklet entitled *Facing Life Alone*.

National Women's Aid Federation, 374 Gray's Inn Road, London WC1 (01-837 9316). Information and sources of help for battered wives, including addresses of local women's refuges.

Jewish Help. There are a variety of organizations specializing in emotional and practical help for Jews. The Jewish Year Book, available from libraries, lists all social work help, family casework services, help for children, grants, and accommodation.

Professional Classes Aid Council, 10 St Christopher's, London W1 (01-935 0641). This council, which helps single parents, investigates individual financial circumstances and advises, refers or gives grants. The education committee provides for children with clothing and (occasionally) school fees, and the council helps with holiday maintenance.

Release, 1 Elgin Avenue, London W9 (01-289 1123). Release, which provides help for single mothers, and legal, medical, and social information, is specially for young people.

6

Don't Use Your Children as Weapons

Perhaps the most difficult thing of all to resolve in divorce is the ownership of joint possessions. Fights over the family silver, books and records are bad enough, but fights over the children are worse. Children, of course, are *not* possessions, a fact easily forgotten in that period of grief between the decision to divorce and the divorce proper. The children become pawns in a game of 'bargain'. 'If you pay me enough child maintenance, I'll let you see Johnny once a week. If you don't, I don't think you should have any rights to him.' Or 'You're leading this carefree new life now with your new woman and no responsibilities, while here I am, stuck at home with the burden of a child. Why should our son get all his treats from you and none from me because I can't afford them? I don't think you should see him.'

Spare a thought for the children. What about *their* rights? What about eleven-year-old Johnny who is *also* feeling bereft, who needs his father just as much as his mother, and who has no understanding of the financial battle which is raging over his head.

'If I hadn't been able to see my father often after the divorce, we'd have lost touch and he wouldn't have been like a father to me,' said one eighteen-year-old boy, whose mother had custody. He was ten at the time of the divorce.

'Seeing my father often is what kept things going; I'd have been very bitter otherwise,' said a sixteen-year-old girl, whose mother had custody. She was eight when her parents divorced.

These are comments from some children of divorce surveyed in Cape Town, South Africa in 1977. One of the questions asked in the survey was 'which parental behaviours were experienced by the child as most distressing?' Over half the children agreed that the most difficult thing they found to cope with was the parents' vilification of each other. Another distressing factor was the restriction of access that the parent with custody might put on the other parent. 'My father is punishing my mother by not letting her see us, but if he's doing this, he's punishing me too.' (A girl of fourteen whose father had custody. She was five at the time of the divorce.)

Some couples begin their divorce with the best of intentions as far as their children are concerned. 'But as our separation sunk in,' says one 34-year-old ex-wife, who has two sons aged five and three, living with their father, 'he began to realize I wouldn't be coming back, that it was truly all over. And the more this dawned, the more it hurt him. He went through a period of sadness, depression, bitterness, extreme anger.

'Although our original agreement had been to share fifty-fifty in the care of our children, he began to make it more and more difficult for me to see them without some kind of a scene. I tried hard to disguise this from the kids but it wasn't easy. I was feeling terribly guilty about leaving in the first place, even though I was sure it was the right decision, and of course I was worried about the children all the time.

'As he felt worse he clung to the kids more. They were his only emotional security left. He was terrified that by letting them spend time with me, they'd prefer me to him and he'd lose them as well as me. The sad thing is that by trying to make me out of bounds to them, he endowed me, in their eyes, with a kind of glamour that made them want to see me more than if the access had been easily available and without dramatic meaning.'

DIVORCE SYNDROME

There is a recognized syndrome of grief attached to divorce, just as there is with death. Its ingredients include pain, sadness, depression, anger, and bitterness. They don't necessarily come to the surface immediately; the separation is often unreal to the partners, or one or both may hope the other will return. When at last it becomes apparent that the other parent isn't going to return, depression and the vindictiveness of anger and bitterness break through.

'You could practically see a cloud suspended over Mum's head, she was that gloomy.' (Max, aged thirteen.)

'I felt as if I was an elastic band. They'd fight over my affections, would get jealous of each other, and my mother was always forbidding me to see my father. She made it very difficult for him. Thank goodness he persevered. He's made all the difference now I'm older.' (Eva, aged sixteen. She was ten when her parents divorced.)

It may be asking the impossible but if the parents in turmoil can understand that they are experiencing a recognized syndrome of emotions which will eventually pass, leaving them more normal, they might be able to swallow some pride and repeat to themselves, 'I must not hurt my children because I am suffering.'

The realistic way to cope is to treat grief as an illness, something unpleasant but temporary. In the meantime, life must be allowed to move along much as usual. Part of this means not subjecting the children to verbal battles, not denying them access to a loved parent and not using them as bargaining points.

FINANCIAL CONFLICT

One of the factors that escalates difficulties between divorcing parents is a financial struggle. It is difficult enough maintaining one family (that is, one household) on today's income; it is so hard to maintain two households on the same income that people often cannot afford to divorce. And those who do invariably find that their standard of living has dropped with a clang. More than half of all single-parent families in this country are at present on the poverty line. Although all parents with custody of their children are awarded child maintenance, they don't necessarily have any other income awarded. And whatever is legally awarded, there is of course no guarantee that it will actually be paid.

In 1978, the National Council for One Parent Families carried out a survey of 126 families on their case files. The families surveyed came from all over the country. Of these, 88 per cent should have received maintenance but only 58 per cent actually did so. Everyone surveyed would have liked a one-parent family benefit which they felt would give them financial security.

Non-support is often used by mothers as a reason for preventing access. The rationale is that if the fathers don't want to care for their children financially, they can't care for them very much emotionally and therefore shouldn't have any rights. It is often hard to separate financial from emotional difficulties and it's a distressing problem to impose upon the kids.

American research indicates that the degree of financial stress the separating parents find themselves in relates directly to the amount of stress there is upon the family. The children who appear to survive divorce best have parents who are not only emotionally mature people but who are able to behave in a way that is financially mature. Mothers who had jobs *before* their marriage ended tend to cope better with divorce than do mothers who were financially dependent on the father during the marriage. This latter group have to make the adjustment not only to being a single parent but also to going out into a business world to earn a living. Another factor is that the woman who is already working will be further up a career ladder than a woman who is only just beginning; she will be earning more and will have better job prospects.

Salaries make working mothers more economically independent of their ex-husbands, of course, but a job also provides a work satisfaction which deflects the focus of grief. Pain and bitterness are assuaged in the woman by the feeling that at least she can be a useful wage-earner. Many women who have never worked during marriage find that fights over child maintenance and their own maintenance become the crux of their broken family life and add to the depression and difficulties they are experiencing. Naturally, their bitterness rebounds on their children. We have all heard the story of the child who says during her visit to her father at the weekend, 'Mummy says I've got to take a cheque home with me tonight or I can't come and see you again.' A telling argument perhaps for the wisdom of establishing some sort of a career *during* marriage and not waiting until a possible divorce.

In 1976, twenty fathers with custody were interviewed and it is significant that although they all agreed their lives had become more difficult, not one of them felt any doubts about their capacity to combine earning a living with bringing up children.

It is, of course, not easy for women to work as well as to bring up children in a country that makes little practical provision for working mothers. Until anti-sexual discrimination is given realistic backing in this country, it will be very hard to find a group of twenty single mothers who unanimously feel the same.

THE NEW EXTENDED FAMILY

A third factor which affects the way in which we cope with divorce is the community in which we live. In earlier days, couples tended to settle near relations to bring up their families, often in a small town or village where the whole family had lived for generations. This meant that there was a relation or a near neighbour who could be relied on to give help with the children if it were needed. Trends since the Industrial Revolution have been to move out of small communities and into towns where there was work in industry. Such moves have led to an uprooting and a loss of ties, which inevitably means loss of support. The old extended family has become a thing of the past and families are now 'nuclear' ones, isolated amongst a crowd of other small families.

When a 'nuclear marriage' breaks down there is therefore less likelihood of family support and more possibility that the parent with custody is going to experience unrelieved stress. Because of the psychological 'conditioning' that mums have had drummed into them over the last thirty years, thanks to child 'experts', childcare has been considered the 'mother's job, the mother's responsibility'. This has meant that Dad has been excluded from childcare until recently. And if Dad hasn't had the opportunity to get in some kind of first-hand childcare himself, this is another factor which aggravates the fight between parents over children.

On the one hand, the mother without extended family support still feels it is her job to look after the children and is now torn between her desire to do this and her need to go out and be a breadwinner. On the other hand, Dad misses his children appallingly, thinks his wife is a cow for making it difficult for him to see them and yet has to admit that he doesn't quite know what to do with them when he's got them.

In my opinion, it is vital that some kind of 'divorce consciousness raising' is begun in this country. With the divorce rate standing at one in four marriages and likely to continue rising, with single-parent families standing at two in five, some hard thinking needs to be done right at the *start* of marriage.

For every four couples making their wedding vows with stars in their eyes and meaning sincerely 'till death us do part', at least one will end up with a broken marriage. It's a fact. If we are following in the American and Scandinavian trend, as we probably are, that figure will eventually become one in three, maybe even one in two. So it would seem to be a 'head in the sand' attitude to embark upon what may well be a temporary arrangement without making practical provision for its end. Most people try and provide for their old age in some way, even if it's only paying towards a state pension, and though the old age pension is a pittance, we have at least arranged our social system so that it exists. Many people take out insurances to guard against pitfalls and problems that won't necessarily but *might* unexpectedly hit them, such as disability, accident, fire, and theft. Many insure their families against the breadwinner's sudden death. But how many of us think of ensuring that our children will be well cared for in the event of divorce? Virtually none.

The fact is, our society is changing. We are no longer a 'single marriage society' but a 'divorcing and re-marrying society'. The sooner we recognize and accept this, the sooner we can begin to make use of what we have got, to help ourselves and our children by extending our families in a modern way. For although Granny no longer lives next door and although our brothers and sisters may be an hour's drive away, there are other ways in which it can be done.

Dinah: 'I work as a part-time teacher which is fine for my

school-age children but difficult for my baby. Luckily for both of us, the mother of a child in my five-year-old's class offered to child-mind and it's worked out wonderfully.'

It may be that your child needs someone to care for him full-time if you are working, which is where a hired help extends your family. If she seems an expensive method of childcare, try finding another working mother in the community who might share her with you.

Anne: 'I advertised in our local paper and asked around local friends until finally I discovered another mother living two streets away who wanted to work. Her child was a year old, my baby was three months. We shared our helper, split the costs between us and incidentally provided the kids with some company for each other which was great when they were a little older because they were both only children.'

Often it's school-age children who are the problem because their hours don't conveniently end with office hours at 6 p.m., but leave them at a loose end from 4 p.m. This is where the community could come in useful. Perhaps there's a parent at your children's school who would take your kids home with hers; if this is not the case, you could advertise for someone – at a local hospital, for example.

Most hospitals have large general notice-boards where members of the public can pin up 'Help Wanted' cards. This type of work may well appeal to hospital domestic staff. With the shift system, they are often off duty by lunchtime and may welcome the possibility of extra income.

Many parents query the effect these additional child-minders will have on their children's lives. If the mother has always had sole care of her children, believing this to be 'right and natural', it probably *will* come as a shock to the children to be separated from her when she has to go out to work after the divorce.

But if they have always been used to others caring for them *as well as their mum*, there will be no dramatic change, and so, hopefully, fewer problems. Hence the emphasis on considering the possibility of divorce when a couple marries, or certainly during the first pregnancy. Mothers can arrange their children's lives so that, right from the start, they include other people who will help care for them.

COMMUNITY CHILDCARE

On the kibbutz in Israel, the children are brought up together in the children's house but spend regular hours with their parents every evening. The peer group is as much a part of the family as the parents, brothers and sisters. This doesn't mean that the parents are devalued in the eyes of the children, nor does it mean that the parents are excluded from the children's lives.

Communal childcare *and* time spent with parents on the kibbutz appears to produce independent-minded youngsters with a well-developed sense of survival and security who still manage to retain an excellent sense of family. Two or more children in the same family learn to rely on each other emotionally, and children brought up together in close relationships, though not actually brothers and sisters, can do the same.

Unfortunately, there are very few communities in this country which raise children in an equivalent way to the Israeli kibbuzim. Yet communal childcare is still not an impossibility.

Research at the University of Sheffield amongst four-year-olds shows that they are capable of accepting several adults to care for them provided these adults are introduced carefully and cautiously, thus allowing the children time to develop trust. Though children are not likely to accept an unlimited number of caring adults, it does seem they can accept between five and ten in the first five years of life without adverse effect, if these relationships are developed properly.

FATHERCARE

And what about Dad? Slowly but surely we are beginning to accept that dads can and should be more involved in rearing. It's good for the whole family. There are moves in this country to arrange paternity leave for fathers; a few individual companies and one trade union have already made provision for it. The law in Sweden allows mothers *and* fathers to divide a year's leave between them to care for a new baby, with a guarantee of their jobs back at the end. To begin with, Swedish males were slow to make use of these arrangements but in the five years since the law was passed, the number of men opting to stay at home with their offspring has increased.

But if the father is so involved with the children, won't he want custody of them in the event of divorce? Well, yes, he may. But isn't it preferable that he should want a warm commitment to his kids, rather than regarding them as an unwelcome responsibility? And as a divorced mother may well have to go out to work it could be welcome and reassuring to know that childcare arrangements can be shared.

So, rather than fighting over custody, why not opt for something that will work out to everyone's advantage – that is, sharing custody? (For further information on custody and how joint custody works, see page 134.)

The concept of shared or joint custody is something not taken up very often in this country. Only 3 per cent of custody arrangements are resolved in this way. But legal authorities investigating the present state of divorce advise that conciliation is desirable. Couples should be helped, they suggest, to talk reasonably together after divorce so that they can come to an agreement over their future living arrangements without friction. Conciliation might well lead to more joint custody agreements between ex-spouses. In The Law Society's recent booklet, *A Better Way Out*, which records the findings of the Family Law Sub-Committee, formal provision for conciliation is one of the most heartily recommended divorce reforms.

THE PSYCHOLOGY OF CUSTODY AND ACCESS

Let us assume, however, that shared care of the children on a fifty-fifty basis is not realistic and that one person has both custody and care and control, while the other has agreed access. Let us also assume, since this is at present most common in this country, that the mother has custody and the father has access.

What can each one do in this situation to alleviate the arguments and differences in which the children are used as weapons?

It is important to begin by understanding that *both* parents go through a period of mourning, not just the partner who has been left. Sometimes the result of this is that the parent with care will see the offspring as representing, on the one hand, a sole remaining security and on the other a burden. So the parent (usually the mother) clings to her family, yet feels under immense strain. She is snappy and bad-tempered with the children, but finds it difficult to let them out of her sight. Yet by letting go, by allowing them to visit friends, grandparents and their father, she will help the children and herself in the long run.

Meanwhile, the father's life has undergone many changes, not all of them welcome, despite his so-called freedom. His accommodation may be uncomfortable, he is probably doing his own cooking, cleaning and laundry – and, worst of all, for the first time in years he's alone.

Though he welcomes seeing his children, they inevitably remind him of happier family occasions and of the recent finale of marital battles and strain. He may therefore focus too intensely on the children. 'He used to just sit and watch Thomas, who was only fifteen months old then,' said one mother. 'It got to the point where he didn't move out of his flat on the weekends he had Thomas. Just wanted to gaze at the child. Of course, Thomas became appallingly bored and not a little disturbed. He needed something more normal.' Although it is very understandable that the father should give his kids concentrated attention on the relatively brief occasions he may now see them, he should try to remember that a young child needs to use up excess energy and becomes bored if there is not much to do.

SENSE OF LOSS

The parent who has moved out may find the sense of loss over his children so intense that he wants to distance himself from them so that he is not constantly reminded of his family life. He may even decide not to see the children at all. But children do need continued contact with their departed parent. So, if he can, the parent should take the view that time will help this sense of loss (though it may never entirely disappear), rather than cutting himself out of his children's lives, a move which he may bitterly regret later.

DEPRESSION

Divorcing parents suffering from depression may find it difficult to cope with the stuff of everyday life – the chores such as housework and cooking. So the children may find themselves struggling through a mess of debris at their mother's house, and visiting an unhomelike new pad which their father hasn't had the energy or the inclination to turn into a home base. These signs of depression become ammunition for embittered spouses. 'Is it wise for him to see so much of the children when he can't even look after himself?' she accuses. 'Won't it hurt the children to be in the care of someone who seems so unbalanced?' he demands.

If each parent can manage to recognize the symptoms of mourning in himself and in his ex, they will both help each other to improve the quality of family activities.

THE CHILDREN'S FEELINGS

It is important for both parents to realize that the children can love each of them separately. Children who are forced to choose between parents are, according to many psychiatric authorities, likely to show destructive feelings in adulthood when they are old enough to have their own families. It needs to be OK to talk freely about the good time they've had with Mum or Dad. If they are afraid to express their experiences with either parent, they will begin to feel insecure, unworthy and mistrustful themselves. The parent who maligns the other parent, and makes it difficult for the children to see him, is forgetting the children's own needs. The children may interpret this as a lack of caring and concern, and stop believing that both parents still love them.

WHOSE RESPONSIBILITY?

Another struggle applies to the parent with access (the father, as we have been using in this example); that is recognition and acceptance that the mother now has the legal and emotional responsibility to raise the children according to *her standards and her philosophy*. If a father cannot accept that this responsibility is no longer his, he makes his offspring's conflict worse.

This acceptance doesn't mean he has to change *his* standards. As already stated, children are quite capable of realizing that different homes demand different behaviours. But it does mean that a father should not directly challenge what the children are being taught by their mother.

It is better to say, for example, 'I know at home your mother insists you're in bed by 6.30. But here we have a rather later bedtime. Your mother and I have different ideas about this,' rather than '6.30 is a ridiculously early hour for bedtime. Your mother's a fool to insist on it. Of course you should be allowed to stay up later.' Strife between children and mother quickly becomes strife between mother and father, all of which heightens the children's distress.

Difference of opinion over bedtime, of course, is only a minor problem compared with, say, schooling and religion, which are major debating points affecting the entire trend of a child's life. It is obviously best if parents can talk to each other to try and resolve differences, but if this is impossible, the parent without custody must accept that these decisions are no longer his. Once he can do so, the tensions between parents will simmer down and the children, both victims and spectators, will be able to breathe more freely.

Sad though it may be, the father with access must also accept that his children's life will revolve around their mother's home which is their primary base, and will unconsciously make choices to ease their life at that primary home. So, if when the children are given a free choice of which home they want to spend time in, they tend to choose the mother's, father should not backbite or complain. It is natural that the rhythm of the children's life should be centred on their main home and it will hurt them if an issue is made of it.

NEEDING THE ABSENT PARENT

Sometimes children seem emotionally insatiable during the time they spend with Dad – they can't get enough of him. In cases like this, one way of toning down the frenetic atmosphere is to *extend* the time the children spend with that parent. It is difficult to cram into three hours the love and affection children might otherwise express over the luxury of a week. But if they know they can spend *more* time with their dad, they can have a more relaxed attitude to these visits. It is the parent with custody, though, who has to allow these extra hours. A mother, with fears of losing her children's affection, may find this a hard decision to come to. If she can accept the idea that the more relaxed the visiting is between children and father, the more secure the children are likely to feel with her, this might help her to be more generous.

It will help no one if the children's real need to see more of their father is viewed as fuel for warfare between the ex-spouses. 'He encourages our daughter to be upset, because it makes him feel more wanted,' says one mother, who is sore about the amount of time she is without her children. 'I consider that he is an emotionally disruptive influence on Jennifer's life. He shouldn't see her so often.' It is hard to tell how much of this is true and how much of it is confused emotion on the part of Jennifer's mother. Either way, the result is conflict for Jennifer. Her parents would benefit from a trip to a child guidance counsellor. And Jennifer's preferences should also be considered, although not allowed to dictate.

It is as difficult for the parent with custody to get used to taking all the decisions at home as it is for the parent with access to realize helplessly that he no longer has control over his children's lives. Each parent resents the situation and blames the other. But whoever is the cause of the problems, it certainly isn't the children, so games of blame and possessiveness have to be kept out of their lives.

If the parent with custody tries to be generous and the parent with access tries to be gracious, they may be going a long way towards improving the after-divorce relationship.

7

Sex and the Single Parent

Most of us have sex urges, and there are those who go so far as to say that sexual instinct shapes our entire lives. However great or small a part it plays, there is one indubitable fact. When you're not getting enough of it, it becomes a problem. And single parents suffer from a specific version of this problem.

Whether or not your sex life was satisfactory with your ex-spouse, one thing was for sure. Sex, once you married, became respectable. It was OK to go to bed with your husband or wife. In fact, it was expected of you. And you got used to it, about two and a half times a week according to some dubious national average. Which means that when you have to do without, you miss it. You miss it partly for its own sake and partly for the sense of value it bestows upon you. You are back in the singles situation of needing to find a new partner with whom you eventually hope to start a sex life (amongst other things) and yet . . . you're not a single. You have one or more little monsters tagging along, who are apt to break in when you are having a cuddle with your new partner and scream ˙for Mummy/Daddy at just *the* most inconvenient time.

And then there's the moral dilemma. Should the children know you have a sex life? If it is all right for them to know, just *how much* should they know? It's one thing dangling a nice steady friend in front of them but it's quite another when you're dating five people in one week or a new friend every fortnight. Should they be let in on any of this or none of it?

Will the children suffer if they learn the truth? Or will they remain totally unaffected? If they find out you have locked the bedroom door one afternoon, what are they going to feel? Come to that, what are *you* going to feel, hearing their shrill demanding little voices from the fleeting luxury of the ex-marital bed? How important is your privacy? Are you entitled to *any*? And what about the children's space? Is that being trespassed upon by the inclusion of Mummy's/Daddy's friend at the breakfast table next morning?

Individual people have individual solutions to these questions. They range from being flagrantly open about sex to celibacy. The answer for most of us, I imagine, lies somewhere in the middle.

MARSHALL

Marshall is a 42-year-old accountant with custody, care and control of his three teenage children. Six years ago, when his marriage broke up, the children were all under eleven. Marshall's strong Christian beliefs influence his lifestyle. He is a just man, although passionate to a point where sometimes his views become distorted. He puts the spiritual welfare of his children above material welfare but also believes in giving them as much independence as is possible.

Marshall's strong sense of morality dictated, when his marriage first ended, that he should provide the children with an alternative mother as soon as possible. With this end in mind, the next time he fell in love he promptly moved his girlfriend in. 'The sex was wonderful,' he said, 'But nothing else was. I'd expected far too much from her. She was twenty-five, a very nice person, but she found the children a struggle. After two years of trying to make it work, we parted in an almighty explosion.

'Apart from leaving me distressed yet relieved, it posed some tricky questions. I did not think it would be good for the children to go through that again. I certainly wasn't prepared to start living with someone again for some time, but I am easily attracted to women. I don't like the idea of going to bed with someone yet excluding her from the rest of my life. So I found myself in a dilemma. As I saw it, I was faced with a choice: to dislike myself by using women in outside sexual relationships, to disturb the children by possibly going through something similar, or to do without sex at all.

'I should say that during my relationship with my girlfriend, the children, slightly to my surprise, adjusted very easily to the new presence in the family – I now know they took an exceedingly sanguine view of my emotional and sexual needs. Little does one realize how well one's children know one! I have always been open in my discussion about sexuality and in my reading matter concerning sex. The children took our relationship and explosive break-ups in their stride, bless them, and pulled me through the crisis. But that didn't alter my feeling that it wouldn't be desirable to subject them to it all over again.

'What eventually happened was that my sex life wound down gradually. I didn't instantly cut all possibilities of sexual relationships out of my life. I love women and, in the event, did become sexually involved with a few more. But I have learnt how to live happily on my own (without a woman, that is), how to conquer loneliness, how to live for each day, how to survive without a woman and, latterly, without sex. I don't know what people make of me and I don't really care very much.

'Most women seem intensely curious and not a little puzzled by it all; I'm aware that it's a highly attractive set-up to many of them, though the slightly cautious ones interest me more and I'm not *desperate* for a mate. Yet the company of women is one of the joys of my life. I am content to hope they like, me. I really don't feel I have anything further to prove, and I've a sneaking suspicion that single-parenthood was the best thing that ever happened to me.'

DON

Don has joint custody of his young sons (aged four and six at the time of divorce). They live most of the time with him and when he was first divorced he employed a full-time housekeeper to help care for them. His house is designed so that his bedroom is on the ground floor, near to the front door, while the children's rooms are on the top floor near to the housekeepér. This ensures a certain amount of privacy for Don. But, as he said, 'if I really liked a girl I didn't want to just go to bed with her. I wanted to include her in the family. At first, unfortunately, the relationships never quite worked out. There was either something the matter with the girl or with me.

'Immediately after my marriage break-up I found myself dating every female I could lay hands on. I think I was trying to prove to myself that I was attractive, as the departure of my wife had given me serious doubts.

'It got slightly embarrassing bringing a girl home after I'd done it once or twice. The children would interrogate them. Are you going to stay here with our daddy? Do you know daddy's other girlfriends? Do you know Betty, Hetty and Letty? Only the strongest survived that.

'Then came the dilemma of the sexual side to the friendship. It wasn't that I couldn't manage to be private with my girlfriends. Once the children were in bed I could. But I felt most uncomfortable making love with them at home. There was always the possibility of that little rap on the door from one of the kids, "Daddy, Jimmy's fallen out of bed and is crying," and although I didn't particularly care what the housekeeper thought, I was still aware of her presence.

'Then there were the mornings after. What to do with these women? I'm inhibited, a lot more so than my children, probably. In any event, I didn't want them to know these girlfriends had spent the night. My fear was that one of the boys would barge in and see a strange head on the pillow where his mother's had once been. So I used to subject the poor women to the most awful subterfuges. If I really liked a girl I'd stand her outside the front door at half past six in the morning and pretend she'd dropped in for breakfast on her way to work. The children swallowed that one. If I wasn't that keen, I'd whip out of bed at two in the morning and drive her home. It didn't please her and it certainly didn't grab me. I needed all my sleep in order to cope with an exacting job and two affectionate but demanding little boys. On top of this, I can see now that I was very depressed. Everything had gone wrong at the same time. My wife had left me, my previous job had folded and I had had to move house, so things were tough.

'Needless to say, all this standing outside the front door at 6.30 a.m. didn't exactly endear me to these favoured women friends and I found myself without them rather smartly. Which was depressing when I really liked them. However, I stuck to my principles because I felt strongly that the kids needed safeguarding. Perhaps I thought *they* would think they were losing my affection by seeing me give it to someone else. In any case, I wasn't taking any risks.

'This went on for the best part of two years. A good result of it was that I developed a very happy and close relationship with the children. We spent a lot of time together. I became more involved with them and more appreciative than I had been before their mother left.

'The tireless dating slowed down after the first six months and I took things (and women) rather easier. When I met the first one who appealed to me in every way it suddenly seemed perfectly natural to include her in my life. She understood my inhibitions about our sex life – indeed, she shared them. Suddenly I lost mine. I didn't mind if the boys did see me with her. I was so proud of her I wanted them to be, too. I was very happy for them to see me with her day and night. After we'd known each other for four months she moved in with us. Although there was never any pretence that she was their mother, she immediately became their stepmother in spite of our not being married. She just naturally merged into our family, which was another reason why I cared for her so much. After we'd lived together for two years we married. She was the first woman I was happy to be found in bed with.

'Looking back, I suspect I need not have been nearly so concerned for the children. I think they knew a lot of what was going on anyway. But I didn't want to take the risk of hurting them more.'

BRENDA SILVER

Brenda's baby, Matthew, was eighteen months old when her husband left her. Unable to afford her flat, she moved back home to her parents. Living conditions were crowded so Matthew shared her room. They continued to live there until Matthew was thirteen, when Brenda remarried.

'I've always been an independent woman,' she says. 'I didn't want to get remarried just to provide a father for Matthew. I could have done that several times over. I wanted to marry to please me or not at all. But all the same, Matthew had to come into it. It would obviously have been pointless marrying someone who was at war with my son. Which meant that an awful lot of men crossed my life until it finally happened.

'And sex was one hell of a problem. There was no way I wanted Matthew to see a succession of "uncles" in and out of my bedroom. Even though I was able to get a lot of privacy, my parents were still around. I used my room as a bedsitting room on the nights I entertained and Matthew would move his bed into my parent's room. But even when my motives were innocent, which was most of the time, I'd feel quite hot under the collar if ever I did have a young man around because I'd be wondering all the time what my mum and dad thought. I am quite a sexy girl so it was all rather uncomfortable. I don't think anyone wants their parents to think of them as sexy. I don't anyway.

'Most of the time, if I was dating, I'd go to the fellow's place. I was fortunate in having my parents as built-in babysitters, and Matthew didn't know about the affairs. There was one man, though, who was very good with children. I did bring him home and Matthew, who was six at the time, adored him. They struck up a wonderful friendship and Peter would just cart Matthew off for whole days on outings. I was very tempted to marry him because of this. But I withstood the temptation. He was very nice but he really wasn't right for me. Even after he and I were no longer going out, he still saw Matthew occasionally. He was a really nice man.

'The reason I was able to last out living with my parents for twelve years was that they did manage to let me have a great deal of privacy, and they also provided stability for my son. My father was a father figure to him, for which I shall always be grateful, and my mother was very patient and helpful to both of us. Of course, it wasn't ideal. I often longed for my own flat but the disadvantages of that would have been hideous.

'Andy started off like any of the others, a good friend whom I also had sex with, at his place. I'd known him for years, from before Matthew was even born. But it wasn't till Matthew was ten that we really got things together. We slowly but surely fell in love. I was very happy to introduce him to my family. He and I took Matthew on several holidays where I made no secret of the fact that I shared a bedroom with him. But back home, he still didn't stay. It just didn't seem right. Or necessary. I got into the habit of staying with him a couple of nights a week and my mother would take Matthew to school on those days. He knew where I was, of course. He had Andy's phone number and phoned me there once or twice.

'Then one summer holiday we all had to get up at the crack of dawn to catch a ferry and Andy stayed overnight with us. He slept with me and Matthew slept in the living room. It seemed the natural thing to do at the time. But thinking about it afterwards I realized that it was a breakthrough. Everyone had accepted him, and so had I. And that's when we decided to marry.'

FRANCESCA

Francesca found herself in a similar position to Brenda. Her second husband left her when their baby was tiny. She moved back into her father's flat when Timothy was a year old. She was fiercely determined never to marry again, and determined to pursue her career in the civil service, even though it was extremely difficult to do so when the baby was young.

'There was no way I was going to be celibate,' she says, 'I love sex although I'm very cautious about long-term relationships with men. That's mostly because I've been unlucky with the men I've picked. They've been marvellous lovers, but lousy husbands.

'It quickly became apparent that I was going to need some privacy. I couldn't take a succession of lovers back to my father's flat. To begin with, I borrowed a friend's flat which I was able to use during the day. At the time that suited me well since I was having a torrid affair with someone who worked quite near me and we used to spend every lunch hour in the luxury of my friend's pad.

'Later on, when I was earning a lot more, I continued to live with my father but also rented my own little batchelor flat. I made no secret of doing so. My son by that time was fourteen and understood the value of privacy. Indeed, he occasionally stayed in the little flat too.

'My father was quite accepting of my independence by then, although he'd given me a tough time in earlier days. He put up no argument about my pad, partly I suspect because he was very anxious that I shouldn't remove Timothy from his home. He has cared for him in his own funny way, and has supplied a fatherly influence which I know has been good for Timothy.

'I can talk to Timothy about anything and that includes my love life. He's sixteen now and is already studying for "A" levels. There haven't been any girls in his life yet because he's been working so hard academically that there hasn't been time for any. His break with us will come when he goes to university, which won't be long now. He's turned out to be a very good-natured, well balanced individual. He's loving and understanding and will make some girl a wonderful old man.'

JACKIE

Jackie was thirty-one when her husband left, and she had three small sons to bring up. Jackie retained the family home and a fixed income for a limited number of years.

'As soon as Mick had moved out, I went out to places where I made quite sure everyone knew I was available. I really needed menfriends to prove to myself I was still sexually attractive. I went a bit mad at first, going from one to another. But then I went on holiday to Majorca and met up with a man I fell passionately in love with. There were an awful lot of things wrong with him, still are. He drinks, and he's married. But he's also very rich and his job entails travelling around the world so he was able to get to England a lot.

'While I was married I'd never even give a thought to the quality of my sex life. I'd just taken it for granted. I'd known Mick since I was sixteen and our sex was always good. It hadn't occurred to me it wouldn't be the same with everybody. But it wasn't. One of the reasons I slept around so much to begin with was that either the men were unsatisfactory lovers or I froze up with them. Either way, it wasn't as enjoyable as it could have been. So when I met Erik and the sex was wonderful, that hooked me. It didn't matter that he was unsuitable husband material, I loved him.

'When he was in England he would stay with me. There was absolutely no secret about the fact that he shared my bedroom. (I'd never brought anyone else back home, mind you.) My two-year-old was an exceedingly poor sleeper and had got used to sleeping with me by them. He didn't take too kindly to finding Erik usurping his place. The result was that Ollie would crawl in with us. We'd wake to find him fast asleep, kicking us while he sucked his thumb.

'But he did become a hazard to our sex life. He seemed to be there in bed with us all the time. We never had a moment's privacy.

'The years went by and the relationship with Erik continued. It was a stormy and passionate one. He behaved appallingly when he was drunk and was an angel sober. One minute he was going to divorce his wife and marry me. The next minute he was back with his wife again.

'I went over and stayed near him in Majorca several times. His wife and I eventually met and managed to make friends. United in the face of the common enemy. He'd mucked both of us around so much we were in very similar situations. He has effectively ended up by having two wives. She has got used to me, and I have accepted that he obviously isn't going to leave her. As long as we both get a fair amount of his time, I can cope. The big threat would be if a third lady came on the scene.

'How has all this affected the children? It's been going on a long time now, about eight years in all. My eldest was ten when I met Erik, and he was already very mature. He'd had to be. I'd leant on him heavily when Mick quit. The middle child I've never got on well with and he is at boarding school which has effectively removed him from much of the drama. The baby has never really known any different. He's spoilt, I grant you that. But he's always been rather special, a souvenir of my husband whom I loved very much. I hadn't wanted Mick to go. But on the surface at least Ollie seems a normal little boy to me. He's boisterous, has got lots of friends and likes all the things that other kids do. He lives on a diet of fish fingers and ice cream, rides his bicycle all over the neighbourhood and does reasonably well at school. He's a lovely little boy.'

CAROLINE

Caroline and Brian have been legally separated for five years. Seven-year-old William lives half the week with his mother and the other half with his father. There have been two main love affairs in Caroline's life since she left Brian.

'I'm a one-at-a-time girl,' she says. 'If only the guys had worked out well I'd have been very happy to get married. Unfortunately, neither of them did.'

Both men in their turn moved into Caroline's home, and so for the years they spent there effectively became William's stepfathers. 'He didn't think much of the first guy but was very keen on the second.

'But William has a good sense of perspective. He sees so much of his own dad that he never thought of either of my lovers as anything other than Mummy's friends. His dad and I are the central figures in his life.

'Of course he's seen me in bed with my lovers. It would have been impossible to avoid and in any case there didn't seem to be any reason for avoiding it. When you live with someone, going to bed with them is part of that relationship and I wouldn't want William to think anything else.

'Now, however, things are a little different. I'm dating four guys at the same time and am going to bed with two of them. So far I've managed to either stay at their places or to have them over on the evenings and weekends William is with his dad. As none of them is really important to me yet, I don't want William to see them coming and going. I don't want William to grow up thinking of me as some kind of a scarlet woman, even if that's what I am. I believe there's a place for discretion in one's sex life and this is definitely it. I also think I'm entitled to some privacy. I wouldn't expect William not to have a love life when he's older, but I don't especially want it thrust under my nose and I don't suppose he would want that either. He's an intelligent little kid now and we have a healthy respect for each other.'

VALERIE

Valerie and Jonathon have been divorced for eight years. Before their marriage broke up they had led a very broad-ranging sex life which included group sex parties and threesomes. Jonathon is a chartered surveyor and Valerie a successful author. You need to be fairly uninhibited to take part in group sex activities and Valerie's lack of inhibition spilled over into her life after the divorce.

She was not backward in inviting attractive young men home to stay the night and there was no question of sneaking them out at three o'clock in the morning. Her children in the early days would come into her room to say hello when they woke up. Greatly to the incumbent's surprise, the children would be formally introduced and would shake hands with him. But there was no need for any confusion he might have felt because the children really did accept the presence of their mother's lovers without batting an eyelid. They would chat to their mother and would then go on down to breakfast.

The children are now aged eighteen and sixteen. 'My son has adopted a half humorous, half cynical attitude towards me,' says Valerie. "Oh, mother and her sex," he's been known to cry. "The well-known sex maniac." He accepts my lovers as a way-out part of my character. Just because I have a zany element doesn't mean to say he is the same. And he isn't. He's a tolerant, easy-going young man with an intelligent sense of humour. He's just about to go to university where I think he will be immensely successful. This last summer has really seen the rise of *his* love life. He fell in love with a girl of his own age and, I'm glad to say, has been quite happy to bring her to our house where I assume they have made love. He has his own room which he now uses as a bedsitting room and what goes on in there is his business and no one else's.

'My daughter is two years younger and is still a little girl in many ways. She spends hours in front of the mirror trying on my clothes. She goes to the local youth club with her girlfriends and is rather giggly about boys. My lovers and her little boyfriends are, as far as she is concerned, on different planes. I don't think she associates her early dating as having anything to do with my early-morning men friends. She's still a virgin although she is reluctant to talk about it. But we have communicated most decidedly about contraception. *She* decided to go on the Pill about three months ago even though there is no immediate need for it. Both her father and I drummed into her the importance of taking responsibility for your own body and for any resulting offspring.

'For the past three years I have mostly dated one man. He spends a great deal of time with us although he also has his own flat. In many ways I'd like to remarry but his age deters me. He's about fifteen years younger than I am and it seems such a big gap. The other lovers have fallen by the wayside. I've changed. Perhaps I don't have the energy for such frenzied goings-on, perhaps I have better things to do. If Paul and I are still together in another two years time maybe I'll think more seriously about marriage.'

TESS

Tess is twenty. She lived with her mother until she was sixteen but kept closely in touch with her father. She moved in with him when she was sixteen and left after a year to live with her boyfriend, Freddie, who she's been with ever since.

'For ten years Dad lived with Mary, whom I liked very much. Of course I knew they had sex together. It was taken so much for granted that I didn't even think about it.

'My father is very open about sex. The reason he split up with Mary is because she couldn't take his bisexuality – he constantly sought out both men and women for affairs. I was sorry for her because I liked her very much but, interestingly enough, I seem to be exactly like Dad. I'm also bisexual and have no desire to confine myself to only one person. I'm very happy to live with my man provided we give each other certain freedoms. I find this easier to do than Freddy does. I happily go to bed with other guys and women but keep Freddy as my main relationship. He can't take that though. It's just like Dad's set-up used to be. I really don't feel jealous though and Dad has become one of my best friends. I know all about his lovers and I'm proud of the fact he feels he can talk in an adult way to me about adult things. Both Freddy and I are very curious about

Dad's love life, actually. I think we feel we might learn something.'

JOHN

John is twenty-two and was brought up most of his young life by his divorcee mother in a suburb of Birmingham. 'Mum was a rebel of her time,' he says. 'She did what she thought was right which was to have long-drawn-out affairs with what seem, in retrospect, to have been totally unsuitable men. She declined to remarry, even though one of her suitors was a terrific fellow whom I adored. I've always missed having a father around. I can remember passionately wishing I'd got a father like the other kids.

'She didn't bring a lot of men to our home, but I was aware they were around. When I was thirteen she seemed to be out an awful lot at night. I didn't like it. I didn't like being left on my own but I didn't particularly want her to bring her menfriends back home. I suppose I was difficult and resentful after her affair with Tony fell through. Tony was the one fellow she did bring home to stay. He lived with us for nearly two years and I liked everything about him. Yes, of course he slept with my mother. Who else would he have slept with?

'I cannot subscribe to my mother's theories of freedom and liberation. She can call it what she likes, I call it sleeping around. She did bring someone else home after she bust up with Tony. It wasn't the sex I resented so much as the assumption that this stranger ought to be welcomed by me. I didn't want her "modern" ideas of living. I wanted a father. And, in particular, Tony.

'I suppose I haven't really forgiven her yet. I left home as soon as I could afford to and I live very differently. I'm going out with a nice girl I met at the Young Conservatives and we are saving up to get married. I think my mother is upset by the fact that I hardly see her now. But since she's just gone off on her fourth pilgrimage to India with some long-haired freak who's young enough to be my brother, I can't believe she's grieving too badly.'

This collection of case histories demonstrates what a poor idea it is to generalize about sexual 'norms' and the 'right way' to conduct a sex life. Every one of these interviewees coped with it differently. A common pattern amongst most new single parents, though, does point to beginning single life with many lovers, building up self-confidence through them, and eventually to settling down with one special partner. Privacy for both parent and children emerges as vital. Most of the parents insisted their children were more at ease with their new sex life than the parent was. Not all did so, however. And the young man who had adopted a way of life totally contrary to his mother's may be an example of a situation where the mother perhaps has missed her cues. If resentments can be routed out and dealt with early enough, the parent's sex life is less likely to become the focus for the children's distress.

If the children are feeling insecure because their parents have separated, they may also feel that their parent's new lover means they are being rejected too. Show them in little ways that this isn't the case. If the lover gets a lot of cuddles, make sure the children do too.

Whatever you may think about the morals of some of the parents detailed here, it does seem to be those with the least inhibitions about their own sexuality whose children are well-balanced. If you can remember that your child is not likely to be as shocked as you think he will be, perhaps that will enable you to proceed with a little less tension. It is healthy to have a good sexual and emotional life. Starting a new relationship may mean settling down one day with a loving and caring partner. It would be a shame to shut out that possibility.

8

A New Family

Step-relations come in all shapes and sizes. As the incidence of divorce and remarriage increases, more and more children find themselves acquiring new fathers, mothers, grandparents, brothers, sisters, aunts, uncles, and cousins. The family unit that so many of us are anxious to preserve is not only alive and well, it's getting bigger every day. And parenting is no longer the exclusive concern of mothers or fathers, for these new family allies can also play their part in bringing up the children.

How the new relationships work out, however, is another matter. Naturally, the better adjusted 'parents' are likely to be more successful than those with insecurities, who may find the going tough. Organizations are springing up overnight, which lend emotional support to the vexed roles of single parenthood, mothers and fathers without families, mothers and fathers with families. Spare a thought, though, for the poor old step-parents, traditionally the anti-heroes of the fairy story. They have nothing. Their role, a difficult and complex one, remains largely unrecognized. Perhaps it is all part of the whitewashing procedure in which the only concept of the family is one husband, one wife and as many children as the bank manager can afford.

It quickly became apparent, when listening to the trials and tribulations of the step-parents interviewed for this chapter, that they could do with a support group of their own. A number of common problems emerged, and even among the 'successful' step-relationships there was some resentment and anger at the behaviour commonly expected of step-parents. The 'healthiest' step-parents were those who were able to put their feelings across to their spouses. These step-parents usually found that, once their partner understood the problem, they were eager to help.

In 'consciousness-raising' groups each participant takes it in turn to tell his or her own story. The others in the group are able to listen and learn from these experiences, then use the information they receive, and the perceptions these trigger off, to alter and hopefully to improve their lot.

The following stories may act as 'consciousness raisers'. They air the problems and successes that step-parents experience.

PAT AND MARTIN

'I can't wait for the two years to be up,' said Bill, aged seven, 'when Pat and Richard will move out again.' Patricia was his father's girlfriend, destined, little did Bill know it, to become his stepmother. Richard is her five-year-old son and the two years referred to were the remainder of the lease on the family flat _not_, as Bill thought, the brief period Pat would be sharing his home. Pat and Richard, although he didn't understand it, were now permanent fixtures. Pat had been living with Martin, Bill's father, for six months when he made that remark. (Martin has custody of his son.)

Bill also made it clear in no uncertain terms that she 'interfered' with the clothes he wore (she had thrown away his favourite pair of jeans which were worn to shreds and far too small), thought it odd she should insist that he bathed every day, and resented seeing less of his father and more of her. His bored impatience revealed he had been perfectly happy _before_ she joined the family and that her intrusion had displaced him. According to both his father and his teacher, he was an original and creative little boy, but constantly sought attention to the point of disrupting everyone around.

A year later, the new relationship rested in a state of truce. 'Pat's all right,' Bill conceded, 'but Richard's a pain. He's so irritating. I wish he would go.' He had got used to Pat's excellent care – indeed, had struck up a friendship with her –

but he still resented Richard's presence. (As Richard was a much younger child and as he was often silly and whiny, Bill's irritation had some justification.)

A few months later Pat told him that she and Daddy were going to get married. He was genuinely delighted. He felt that at last he was getting back into a proper family and was full of plans for how late he would stay up at the wedding party.

The two years they had spent together served as a probationary period for Pat and Bill. During that time Bill's feelings had swung from dislike to affection. Contained in the relationship were certain aspects which had helped make it change.

Bill had been introduced to Pat gradually. In fact, Martin had known her for six months before they decided to set up house together. During that six months she had been treated as 'Daddy's friend', not as 'Daddy's girlfriend, destined to become Daddy's wife'. Pat had the sense to know that her relationship with Martin did not automatically entitle her to a good relationship with his son. Understanding this, she treated Bill as a separate person and built up their friendship separately.

She also realized it would take time, years rather than months, to create that friendship and did not therefore become despairing when, on occasions, she was faced with a very rude, disobedient little boy.

She was patient with his rages, recognized his feelings of insecurity and did not force the friendship. She was aware she could never take the place of his own mother and did not insist that he looked on her as such. She also came to terms with being unable to feel the same way towards Bill as she did towards her own child. Fortunately, she was able to behave justly towards Bill even though the behaviour did not come spontaneously.

Pat managed to make friends with Bill's natural mother (who had access) and shared child-caring arrangements with her. Bill's happiest times were when both 'mums' got together with him for a chat.

With both parents *and* step-parents co-operating, Bill had an ideal emotional back-up to rely on during the early difficult days of learning to live in a 'new family'.

SYLVIA 'ET AL'

Jason, also aged seven at the time of divorce, was provided with an 'alternative' family life so different from the one he had enjoyed during his parents' marriage that its novelty cushioned the impact of separation. Sylvia, his mother, moved into a country farmhouse where she and Jason lived as part of a community. They joined six adults and five other children. Her new manfriend was a member of the community but lived there separately from Sylvia. Jason acquired five new 'brothers and sisters' (from three separate families) and six new 'parents'. Bunny, Sylvia's manfriend, assumed little more importance in his life than the other adult members of the group. Jason's natural father, Dave, visits infrequently but when he does, he spends weeks at a time with his son.

Three years later Jason is busy and occupied with his friends and his role in the community. At community meetings, which take place once a week, he gets a say with everyone else. His fears and worries are taken very seriously, not only by Sylvia, but by all the adults.

Two of the adults in the community play a particular part in Jason's life. His interests are centred on the farm animals (the community is run as a small-holding) and he plans to expand the money-making side of the farming. At ten he proudly keeps an eggbook and a milking book in which he records the amount produced and the prices fetched. He confides most in Jeremy, the full-time farmworker, and is already planning to go to agricultural college, and follow in Jeremy's footsteps.

Jenny is the woman who cares for Jason when Sylvia goes away from time to time. She is the community's cook. On Tuesdays when she fetches him from school he helps her in the kitchen (the other children help on other nights, if they want to). He is very proud of his culinary efforts, is capable of cooking a three-course meal and shares with Jenny a zany sense of humour which extends outside the kitchen. The two of them have a theatre project where they put together a knockabout show every so often for performance at one of the community evenings.

When he and Sylvia first moved in, Jason was, not surprisingly, confused. He had come from a conservative two-parent family living in a suburb of Manchester, to a busy farmhouse in an isolated part of Wiltshire inhabited by a muddle of people. It was the community routine and the 'special' friendships he made which nurtured his new sense of security and helped him make a considerable readjustment.

Jason has effectively selected his own 'step-parents' (Jeremy and Jenny) on the basis of shared interests. He is happy to spend more time with them than with his own mother. Jenny and Jeremy both like the special friendship that has grown up between them and Jason, and each shares with Sylvia any talking point or problem concerning Jason that they consider needs attention.

The only real long-term problem lurking in the background is the possibility that Jenny and Jeremy may move on elsewhere. Communities tend to get a high membership turnover. However, since most of *these* community members are parents, they were able to agree on and establish a settled background and stable relationships for the children. On the rare occasions that newcomers are considered, they are put through some heavy questioning about their future aims which forces them to examine their commitment to the community, and especially to the children, very seriously. The result so far has been that very few of the adults have moved away and all the children have remained. The children appear to be happy and healthy and benefiting from the rare environment which is their home.

JOY AND JULIAN

Less unique, perhaps, as an example of step-parents but more relevant to most of us is Joy and Julian's family. They have five children between them. Joy's two live with her and Julian, while Julian's three live with his ex-wife.

'Julian's children are older than mine,' explained Joy, 'So Julian had to regress in order to cope with my kids. He was used to older children and you soon forget what it's like when the children are babies.

'I explained carefully to my two that Julian's children were very important to him because he was their daddy and that they, my children, were very important to their own daddy. They understood this but they still found it hard to make do with less of Julian's attention when his children were around. And they did object to the double standard of manners which he practised. He would be heavy and Victorian with my kids – over not speaking with their mouths full, for example. Yet when his kids, on the one day in the week that they visited us, did the same, he didn't tell them off. My children, not unnaturally, thought this was unfair. But Julian was in a dilemma. He didn't want to spoil the rare and precious time he spent with his three by bellowing at them. I explained this to mine but they didn't like it.

'Far from Julian and the children being jealous of each other, the children were actually jealous of me. I can remember Abigail, aged three, firmly sitting between us on the sofa and pushing me away. She wanted Julian to herself.

'It was Abigail who invited Julian to live with us. I hadn't let him move in because I was worried about what my friends and relations would say. But Abigail and Mark grew more and more concerned every time he left us to go back to his flat. They had visited the flat once or twice. "Aren't you lonely?" Abigail would ask him. "Poor Julian. It's cold at his flat. Can't he stay here?" She even offered him the spare bed in her bedroom. Eventually I decided I was being silly. I asked the children if they would mind Julian moving in. They were delighted. Abigail made a point of telling Julian the invitation had come at her request.

'I used to be extremely self-conscious when Julian cuddled me in front of his kids. I'd try and wriggle away but he wouldn't let me. "They'll see," I used to gasp in horror. "I want them to," he replied. "I want them to see that I love and value you. It's important." Thinking about it now, he was absolutely right. And I can see that, particularly in cases where one partner was constantly under-valued by the ex-partner in front of the children, it is very constructive for the children to see that their parent is loved and is therefore worthy of love.

'Julian has a short, sharp temper. I used to worry when he bellowed at the kids for some small misdemeanour. But minutes later both he and they have forgotten. Kids have amazing resilience if they like someone. They just accept his behaviour pattern. *I* find it much harder to get used to.

'I fall into the trap of being *over* concerned about his relationship with them. Once, when he'd bawled Mark out about something, I screamed at him. "How dare you talk to my kid like that. That's not your child, you can't do that." We yelled at each other all the way up the road till he finally stopped and asked Mark, "Are you upset with me?" Mark turned round and vaguely asked, "Why?" which completely flattened me. The child had already forgotten about it.

'It's much easier for Julian to be a stepfather to my kids, whom he lives with and has known since they were quite young, than it is for me to be a part-time stepmother to his kids. To them I'm a parent but not a real one. I'm not part of their life, yet I'm sometimes asked to assume complete control of them. This can be very hard to do.

'Once, when we all went on holiday to Portugal, one of the girls began to cry. No one knew what the matter was, no one could get any sense out of her, until a suspicion crossed my mind. "I want a private word with you," I said to this thirteen-year-old.

' "Have you just started a period?" Tearfully she nodded. "Have you ever had one before?" No, she hadn't. "Did your Mummy pack the necessary equipment?" No, she didn't.

'So there we were, on a Sunday, in a foreign country with every chemist shop tight shut, with a child who wasn't mine going through a major physical event in her life. I was quite unprepared to deal with it.

'We managed but it wasn't easy. I explained about not swimming, made extensive use of some cotton wool and bought some STs first thing next morning. Julian was 50 per cent worse than useless. He retreated to the centre of the swimming pool where he stayed half the day.

'I can't adapt as effortlessly to step-parenting as Julian apparently can. He is convinced, rightly or wrongly, that his feelings for all the five children are now the same. He means this. It's very nice for my children but not so nice for his. I suppose it's his reaction to feeling he's lost his girls and so he has transferred some of his affection to my kids. I know very few people in similar circumstances who can truthfully say the same.'

JUDY AND DEREK

Judy from Edmonton told her story briefly on my local radio phone-in programme. Her new husband's relationship with her five children was poor. 'Derek is eight years younger than I am,' she explained, 'and only ten years older than my eldest kid. He has no children of his own and has little patience with mine. He loves my little one (a boy, aged five) but is very unpleasant to the others. The eldest (aged sixteen) won't speak to him and says he's going to leave home.'

Derek expected Judy to serve him meals before the children sat down to the table, even when the little ones were starving. While the eldest child was studying for 'O' levels, the stepfather insisted on carrying out some very noisy home improvements. 'There was no need for him to do the building work then,' complained the distressed mother, 'it did seem as though he'd picked that particular time just to be a nuisance.'

He complained he was paying for the children's education when they should be out earning a living. He used this as an excuse to run down their own father for not contributing more. 'This wasn't even true,' said Judy, 'because my ex-husband has agreed to pay for their further schooling. But he's managed to make my two eldest feel guilty about being intelligent enough to want to stay on at school.'

Judy rapidly catalogued a number of unpleasant truths about her new husband that demonstrated three things very well. Firstly, that her husband sounded very young and insecure. A ready-made family of five children must have been extremely daunting for him and the result had been to bring out the worst in his nature in a panicky attempt to show who was boss. Secondly, that it is very easy to alienate people over small yet all-important domestic arrangements, and thirdly, that people like Derek, marrying into a ready-made family, need some kind of advance education on how to deal tactfully with step-families.

Ironically enough, Judy had not called to ask for help with her husband, but to seek advice about whether it would be a good idea for her new husband to formally adopt the youngest child!

JANET

Janet was thirteen when her mother, Marion, remarried. 'It was quite obvious I was in the way. They'd be cuddling on the sofa and would jump apart nervously if I went into the room. They seemed to have some sort of a constant private joke that they wouldn't let me in on. It got to the stage where Charlie would make pointed remarks about "your brat" to my mother. By then I'd become so angry and upset I was pretty obnoxious in return. I know my mother felt very concerned about me but she'd made the mistake of falling in love with a real bum. She was powerless. She couldn't force him to like me and be nice to me.

'It wasn't that he was cruel or even consciously unkind. But he was thoughtless. He'd make plans that didn't include me and then react unpleasantly when he was reminded I'd be there too.

'My way of coping with this was to pull out. I found myself a steady boyfriend and went out every night to escape the tension at home. I'm sure my work at school suffered from it. I'd been quite bright. The teachers had said I stood a good chance of going on to do "A" levels but all I wanted to do was leave as early as possible and get a job so that I could leave home. I did get some "O" levels but left school at sixteen and moved into a flat with three other girls almost immediately. It was awful leaving my mother. She was very upset by my departure. The marriage wasn't working out too well (he left her a year later) but by that time I had to think about me. I needed some peace.'

Janet married at eighteen. 'Ironically, I could have moved back to my mother's house then because she was living on her own again. But I'd met Sean.' The marriage to Sean didn't work out but since she and Sean didn't produce any children Janet feels that neither had anything to lose by splitting up.

Could her relationship to her stepfather have been any different? 'We both needed things explained to us; neither understood that the other need not be a threat. We must both have been excessively insecure. I don't think, looking back, that Charlie was an unpleasant man. He just knew nothing about teenage girls. He didn't have a clue that I might be upset because my own father had left us or that I thought he (Charlie) was to blame. He had no insight.

'I was at a stage of adolescence where all my feelings were heightened. It wasn't difficult to slight me, practically anything would make me fly off the handle. I can see now I would have been difficult to cope with, even for my own father. My rudeness and aggressiveness must have seemed to Charlie as though I was trying to push him away from my mother. I suppose I was. Instead of understanding and being patient, he pushed right back. Result – a nasty, rebellious, unhappy girl. The sad thing is that if he and I had been able to get on better I think my mother's marriage to him would have had a better chance. It's my mother who ended up the loser. She has no one now.'

LOSSES

Remarriage forces the children of divorce to accept the finality of their parents' separation. They have to face the end of their fantasies that Dad will return to Mum and all will live happily ever after. And if the remarrying parent goes to the altar soon after the separation, he/she is not giving the children much time to get over the shock of the marriage break-up. Thus the children are subjected to even more trauma.

Relatively little is known about a child's susceptibility to grief. Some psychiatrists believe that children are incapable of mourning, therefore a child's grief may be put off, spun out or avoided. Since all this may be prolonged over several years, and since the average time between divorce and re-marriage is three years, the children may, at that late date, still be grieving. A residue of sorrow will make it harder for them to accept a step-parent.

Remarriage alters the structure of a family. The fact that, overnight, a whole new set of relations is acquired forces the children to see themselves differently. The eldest child may find that she is no longer the head of the siblings, the youngest child, used to being spoilt as the baby, may find to her dismay that a new 'baby' has appeared on the scene. The younger child, used to being the buddy and support of her eldest sister, may find herself pushed out in the cold while the elder sister concentrates her companionship on a new stepsister. And of course, there is a whole new array of stepcousins, aunts, grandparents.

Jill Thiess, an American social worker, argues that remarriage is a 'potential crisis event in the life of a child, which parallels divorce in significant ways'.

A new stepmother or stepfather may intensify the children's feelings of loss over the departed parent. While the parents are able to gain new spouses, the children cannot gain a new mother or father.

If the children have lived alone with their single parent for some time, they may resent the 'intrusion' of a step-parent and will jealously try to come between the new partners. Feelings of helplessness will be reinforced by not having the natural parent to turn to.

A final loss in some families is where the children discover they are expected to forget about the natural parent and accept the new parent as a substitute. The studies of Kelly and Wallerstein in the United States demonstrate this type of distress and stress the importance of continuing the access to the departed parent as an aid to the children's acceptance of remarriage and a step-parent.

Yet relating to two fathers or two mothers may pose some tricky questions too. Can I love two fathers? If I love one of them, will it mean the other feels rejected? Worse still, if I love one of them will the other reject me?

As some of the previously related case histories show, it is possible, with time and careful handling, to feel comfortable with two families.

GAINS

Remarriage often provides stability and a feeling of caring that the children have been forced to live without during the years of separation. The new relationship may provide a better model of caring and loving than has been available before. If the natural parent has previously been suffering from depression, the arrival of the new spouse will remove the bad feelings and lighten the entire household. Without detracting from the qualities of the departed parent, the step-parent may fit well into the children's lives, may be more knowledgeable about their special interests, may provide a new dimension. Some people are naturally better parents than others. It could be that a step-parent is an improvement over the natural parent. But this doesn't have to pose a threat to the natural parent; there is room for both.

We know it is possible to enjoy a good family life in a remarriage; we know it is possible to continue a happy and loving relationship with the parent with access; we are becoming aware that flexible access to both families is best for the children concerned. Yet Jill Thiess makes an interesting and important observation. She writes in a paper published in the US *Journal of Clinical Child Psychology: Vol. VI, No. 2, Divorce: Its Impact on Children:*

> Adults in our society increasingly reject the concept of permanent monogamous marriage by insisting upon the freedom to love whom they please. This freedom has not been extended to children for they are still governed by a belief system that teaches and allows them to love only their own kin. This belief system has become a double standard for children and upon remarriage it becomes a double bind. How can a child accept remarriage when he has been inculcated with a belief in permanent marriage and enjoined to love and trust only his natural parents? Adherence to this belief system is an overarching factor in remarriage as a situation of loss and conflict for children rather than a source of positive gains and security.

> Divorce and marriage lay bare society's childish attitudes and dramatise further the inadequacy of our institutional provisions for continuity in parental care and love of children. Enabling children to emerge from divorce and remarriage with their capacity to love and be loved intact is an awesome effort requiring not only individual change but also institutional reform.

At the moment we are having to make do with individual change. That change begins at home, inside the family, between parents and step-parents.

How the Change is Brought About
- By introducing the new step-parent gradually, giving him or her a chance to make friends with the children.
- By making it clear that the inclusion of the step-parent does not mean the exclusion of the children, then following that through.
- By continuing to play an active part in the children's lives and not dumping them in the step-parent's lap.
- By allowing the step-parent to acknowledge that he/she is *not* their natural parent and therefore cannot feel the same kind of love.
- By letting the children know the departed parent is still important to them and by allowing them as much access as is desired by all concerned.
- By backing up the step-parent on questions of discipline, having first made sure you and he/she agree generally about the children's upbringing.
- By continually comparing notes about discipline, both with each other and with the parent with access.

PROBLEMS

Q I cannot like my two step-children. I feel extremely guilty about this and fall over backwards to be nice to them. But they really are little brats. I've been married to their father for six months now.

A Six months is too short a time in which to expect stepchildren to adjust to their new parent. Behave kindly but firmly to them. Don't overdo your patient behaviour, however. It's time they began to modify their behaviour and think of your feelings as well as their own. Make it clear that you are a human being too and as such deserve some consideration. It may take between six months and three years for their feelings about you to settle down. If you can understand that they have had a lot of unpleasant changes to put up with in the past, perhaps you can manage to bear with them.

The children may well be feeling their mother is rejecting them in favour of you or that they resent you for usurping (as they see it) the role of their father. There is no rule that says you *have* to like your stepchildren, though obviously it makes caring for them easier if you can manage it. If you are able to satisfy your conscience that you are giving them the best attention they could get from you, then you are doing a good job. There is of course nothing to say that the children must like you either. They are entitled to their opinions, and their opinions have to be accepted.

Bear in mind that your behaviour now is setting a pattern that they will get used to and will therefore come to expect. So don't give in on battles you consider to be important because you feel guilty. If you do they will expect you to continue giving in in the future. Try to assess how much anxiety you think they are still genuinely feeling and how much they are simply playing you for an 'old softie'. But, above all, forget about feeling guilty. The majority of step-parents don't love their stepchildren as their own.

Q I am anxious to make a good relationship with my young stepson. His mother and I have been married for three years and Harry is now aged eight. To begin with I didn't see much of him because he spent a lot of time with his father. Now he's at home with us more often. But I find my wife is over-protective. She's seen him hurt by his father and is terrified I will do the same. The result is that he looks on me with distrust because his mother has unwittingly taught him to do so.

A Your wife's feelings of concern are understandable. But if her separation of you and the child make life difficult for you in your own home, then it's a question of setting some house rules. The home is yours as well as hers and the child's. You should be able to feel you get a fair deal in your own home and should tackle your wife along these lines. There should be certain agreed rules about childcare and it is up to you to work them out with her and to do so in such a way that she will keep to them.

Perhaps agreeing that you should spend specific times alone with the child would be one way of getting closer to him. You could ensure that those times were of real interest by involving him in some kind of work project where he felt he was contributing towards the home in an adult way. If you were the parent giving him this kind of satisfying responsibility, and if you did so regularly, he would begin to see you first of all as a workmate and secondly as someone who allows him to feel free and feel good. Whitewashing a garden wall is one messy but highly rewarding work project. Helping with household carpentry and giving him his own set of tools is another. If you can cook, cake-making, rolling pastry and shape-cutting are perfect for incidentally shaping a better relationship. This will all build up the child's feeling of family.

Q I am concerned that my husband constantly favours his children, often to the exclusion of mine. (We each have two daughters.) If tackled about it, he denies his behaviour and accuses me of being over-sensitive. The trouble is, he honestly doesn't realize he's doing it. The result is that I find myself doing the same with my two, simply because I'm trying to compensate them for his behaviour. I'm sure this will be harmful for the children, giving rise to feelings of insecurity. How can I change things?

A Any child-minder who cares for extra children alongside her own will tell you that it is impossible to treat them equally. Subconsciously, most of us are tuned in to our children's special 'wavelengths' and it is not easy to pick up those of 'outsiders'. So a certain amount of favouritism is not only unavoidable, it's natural. And your own children should be able to accept this. Where such exclusion is harmful is if it is done spitefully or if it is done to excess. Assuming that this is not the case, you and your husband must just keep reminding yourselves to include each other's children. This way, the children won't get too much of a raw deal. I don't think it is a good idea, incidentally, to favour your children *in retaliation* for your husband's behaviour. It may seem unfair, but two wrongs don't make a right.

If your husband's exclusion of your children *is* done spitefully and if talking does not change his attitude, then you are put in the painful position of having to make a choice. There are three alternatives. The first is that you do nothing and your children suffer. Second, that you think seriously about getting the children's natural father to have custody of them. And third, that you decide to set up a separate household from your second husband. None of these is pleasant but if your husband constantly subjects the children to unkindness, you are already in an unpleasant situation. Unpleasant situations call for unpleasant remedies.

However, there is the possibility that your husband's behaviour in favouring his children to excess, and sometimes in being spiteful, is a reflection of some unresolved problem he feels he has with you. If this *is* a possibility, you need to talk in depth with him to try and work out a solution. Bringing in a marriage guidance counsellor may be necessary and useful here.

Q I have two sons and my second husband has one. My youngest son, who is used to being my baby, has now had his nose thoroughly put out of joint by the arrival of his stepbrother who is four years younger. He has overnight become a 'middle child' and he doesn't like it. He seems to have regressed. He's been going to the toilet by himself for two years now, yet all of a sudden he appears unable to cope with cleaning himself and has to have me there to do it. I can understand why he's behaving like this but am finding it hard to cope, because inevitably I have my hands full looking after the very difficult and demanding three-year-old stepson.

A It is difficult for your youngest child and, stressful though it is for you, he does need your sympathy. He feels displaced and since he may already have felt rejected by your first husband's departure, perhaps the new stepbrother is adding to those feelings of rejection. Play along with him for a while. If he wants you in the bathroom, make allowances for him and play the game. After all, if he too were a three-year-old you would *have* to be there for him. He'll get over it and will soon think of something better to do.

Perhaps in your preoccupation with the three-year-old you have not concentrated as much as you should have on your son's needs. It might help if you regularly spent a certain amount of time solely with your son. If it is impossible to do this while the three-year-old is around, arrange with your new husband that he takes complete charge of the baby every evening for an hour. That hour could then be devoted to the seven-year-old.

If this doesn't sound as if it would work, arrange for a relative or friend to take the three-year-old out for regular afternoons in the week. This could then be the seven-year-old's 'special' time. If you can keep this up for some months, your little boy should feel more secure.

You can gradually wean him off the special times when he seems able to manage without them. If he becomes upset again, simply carry them on for a little longer. Incidentally, don't leave out the eldest child. Because he behaves happily, this doesn't mean to say he can't feel excluded too.

Q My husband's parents visit us often and every time they come over, they bring little presents for my husband's children. They do not, however, bring anything for *my* kids. This would be all right if my children's own grandparents did likewise, but *they* usually only give presents at Christmas and on birthdays. My children feel this is very unfair and have become jealous of their stepbrother and stepsister. Am I unreasonable to expect these grandparents either to bring something for all of them or not to bring anything at all? I don't want to be mean or unrealistic.

A You are not being mean or unrealistic. The grandparents are probably unaware of the bad feelings they are creating with their gifts and may only need this pointed out to them to reach a satisfactory solution. If they want to give presents to their own grandchildren, of course that's understandable. But ask them if they could include your kids, even if only on a very small scale – say, by bringing them tiny toy cars, or a set of pencils or felt-tip pens.

If they react badly to your (tactful) suggestion, you are quite justified in being polite but firm to them. Explain that you understand their desire to please their grandchildren but that those same children are now part of a larger family. The children's situation has changed, and therefore, so has the grandparents'. If this still does not raise the required response, make it clear that any presents they bring will be regarded as joint family property.

This may not seem very satisfactory but the situation is an unsatisfactory one. The alternative is to have one set of children feeling left out and the other set being spoilt, plus a lot of internal bad feeling which you as their guardian can do without. If you explain your decision about sharing to your stepchildren on the grounds that different sets of people have different rules and that what is right for their grandparents' home is not right for yours, they may not like it, but they will be able to understand it and ultimately accept it. I think it is important that you have your husband's back-up on this issue because if there is ill feeling you don't want to have split sides in your camp.

Q I am about to marry a divorcee with a little daughter. I know nothing about children, particularly little girls. I don't dislike them but just don't have a clue about how to behave. The child is six. I've never been interested in children nor particularly wanted any of my own, although I can see I might change my views on that. Naturally, I want my new marriage to work out and I'm anxious in case I mess it up by being an unsatisfactory stepfather. How should I behave?

A Why not regard making a relationship with your future stepdaughter as you would any subject you were about to study. If you were about to start a new study course or a work project you knew nothing about, you would keep a low profile to begin with and let those in the know do the talking. But you would stick around, picking up as much as you could about the project until you began to feel you had something to contribute. That would be the time to make a move.

Look on your fiancée as the instructor and project-leader. Spend time with her and the child, getting to know the child's interests, likes and dislikes. Be polite to her but if you don't feel you have anything to say, let her mother make the conversation and take the decisions. Ask your fiancée about the girl, find out what her daily routine is. What kind of a school does she go to? What kind of clothes does she like to wear? What does she do after school? Where does your fiancée see you fitting into the routine.

Every child is an individual. Whereas one child may love being taken to the zoo and will respond to discussions about wild life with eagerness, others will turn up their noses at anything so unsophisticated and will instead put on the latest Abba record. It is this sort of detail that your fiancée can fill in.

If your fiancée is expecting you to provide some sort of discipline in the home, explain that you are willing to do so when you have got to know her daughter but that it's early days now and you would feel out of line telling someone who is a stranger what to do.

Don't rush things. The child may be feeling just as nervous as you are. If, after you have lived together for a while, you find some of her behaviour unacceptable (she's rude, she eats with her mouth open, she won't answer you when you ask her something in front of other people), consult her mother. Work out with her the best way of tackling the child.

Certainly she shouldn't be allowed to get away with being rude, but there may be overriding circumstances. As you begin to feel comfortable in your new home set-up, you will feel more confident. When that happens you will feel capable of dealing with your stepdaughter's problems and of making friendly overtures.

Q My young stepchildren come back after weekends spent with their father feeling unsettled and behaving rather badly. My wife is very concerned about them and thinks she should cut down their visiting time to their father. He is very opposed to this and thinks that if any change is made, he should see them *more* often. I sympathize with her and care about the children but . . . they are not mine and I need the regular break from them that I get at the weekends. To tell the truth, I think I'd go spare if I didn't have that little bit of regular time to be alone with Jackie. Our marriage will definitely suffer if this isn't taken into account. I can see this puts Jackie into a dilemma but what alternative is there?

A It sounds as though this is a case for you, your wife and her ex-husband to get together to discuss the children. This may sound a preposterous suggestion, but other couples do it and pool their common experience of the children with satisfactory results. All three of you have a point of view that needs to be taken into consideration. Come to that, so have the children. Your wife should examine her reasons for *not* wanting them to see her ex-husband more often. Could it be she is afraid of losing them? Extra time with their father might after all be a very satisfactory solution. This is where you come in as a support and, may I venture, a consolation. If you make your married life with her so satisfactory that she feels completely secure, she will be able to risk the children staying away longer.

What do the children want? Has anyone thought of finding out? The best person to do this would be someone who is *not* so emotionally involved with them. It just might be a suitable job for you, their stepdad. Children are loyal. They might give each natural parent the answer they know that parent wants to hear, regardless of whether or not it is the truth. But with you, they may say what they really feel.

Perhaps you could try leaving things as they are for a while. It would certainly be a mistake to jeopardize your relationship with your wife. As that becomes more routine and more reliable, both she and the children will settle down. A certain amount of re-adjustment on the part of the children as they switch from home to home is natural. But children can and do cope with this kind of change. Often when it appears unsettling, it is really one of the parents who is unsettled and who is passing on the feelings of anxiety.

If there is genuine cause for concern (the parent with access is neglecting the children or being cruel to them), you must naturally be prepared to rescue them. But if the unsettled feelings stem mainly from coping with the changeover from one household to another, then the sooner your wife can feel calm about it, the sooner the children will adjust.

One of the great difficulties a step-parent has to cope with is the fact that his/her spouse, although divorced from the previous partner, is still very much related because of the children. One of the ways of continuing that relationship after divorce is by continued squabbling with the ex-spouse. This just might be one of those cases. If it is, your wife needs some counselling so that she can talk through her feelings. You are not necessarily the person with whom she should do this, since you have a vested interest in steering her off the subject. Encourage her to consult a marriage guidance counsellor. She might feel a lot better for it. And so, indirectly, would the rest of the family.

Q My husband very much wants me to have a baby. He has no children of his own but I have two sons from a previous marriage. I would quite like another baby but it's not on my list of priorities. I can understand, however, just how important it is for him. My main hesitation is based on my concern for my two boys. How are they going to react to a little half-brother or sister? Is it going to be very disturbing for them and heap anxieties on top of those already arising from the divorce? Is a new baby a wise move?

A It is unlikely that your children would be so disturbed by the advent of a new baby brother or sister that they would be seriously harmed for the rest of their lives. They certainly might suffer the inconvenience of a tired mother and an irritating junior member of the family, but eventually the tiredness stops and the baby grows up.

Every child fears displacement by the birth of a new baby, and some displacement is inevitable. When you have a tiny helpless infant which needs constant attention, you simply cannot spend as much time and energy on the older children as they have been used to.

The real question is, will it exacerbate any insecure feelings the children may have stemming from the divorce? It is impossible to give a general answer because so much depends on what the divorce was like and how settled the children's background is now.

If you, the children and their stepfather have been living a settled life together for the past couple of years, and if there is a minimum of conflict between you and their father, then the odds are that the children will react to the baby much as they would if you were still married to their father and the baby was a full sibling. If, on the other hand, your divorce was fraught with drama, the separation has been noteable for the fights with your ex, and the children have been relentlessly used as weapons, then yes, they might be upset. They will probably have learned to distrust most of the moves made by their parents. You are the only person who can ultimately decide on extending your family.

Q My husband has custody of our two daughters (mutually agreed) but they spend a great deal of time with me and my new husband; about two-thirds with my ex-husband and one-third with me. The problems arise from the relationship of my girls with my new partner. He is their stepfather but doesn't really feel like one because the girls don't actually live in our home. He has occasional contact with them and is therefore expected to share those occasional parts of their lives. Yet he has no real rights of control, which means he feels ineffective and superfluous. Naturally, he dislikes this and tends to opt out of their lives altogether, which distresses me as nothing would please me more than for us all to play happy families together.

A You can't force anyone to enjoy a relationship and the kind of part-time stepfather you have just described has a tricky role. Perhaps you should work out two things. The first is to make it clear to the children that there are rules and regulations in your home and they have to abide by these, just as they have to abide by their father's rules in his house. If this is also discussed with your husband, the children will receive a framework inside which they can live their lives in your household and, your new husband, knowing what that framework is, can feel more comfortable. To do this, you must talk to each other about the children regularly between their visits, so that he knows exactly where he stands with them on their visiting days.

Secondly, although you can tactfully keep trying to involve your husband in your family life, if this continues to be unsuccessful, you must accept that he and the children will have to spend most of their time apart. This may hurt you, and it may disillusion you about his family sensibilities. But you will have to incorporate his lack of involvement into your lifestyle. This is not an excuse for bad behaviour on his part, of course. Certainly you have every right to expect him to be polite and kind to the children on the occasions they meet. But you would be sensible to plan your activities with the children without including him. Over the months, he will grow more used to them. He may even join in your activities eventually. But he certainly needs time to get used to them and their lifestyle. Meanwhile, you have got to think of your life with them and organize it so that it is satisfactory.

As the parent with access, you may find you are trying to re-create the kind of family life you had together before the divorce. While you can enjoy the *new* family lifestyle you now have, you need to come to terms with the fact that the old family no longer exists, and therefore the old family lifestyle cannot either.

Q My three stepchildren have firm ideas about my role in their lives. They see me as responsible for the break-up of their mother's marriage. They are quite right to think this but ignore the circumstances which led to their mother wanting a new relationship in the first place. (She found their father a most unsatisfactory husband.) They choose to think of me as an unfortunate fad in their mother's life and not worthy of serious attention. I find it extremely annoying when, in front of others, I say something to one of them and find myself ignored. They pursue this to the point of rudeness and I can't see any likelihood of change. Their mother is extremely upset by it but has been unable to change them. The oldest boy is eighteen and is shortly to go to university, the other boy is sixteen and is already out at work, while the girl is thirteen and still at school.

A It sounds as though your stepchildren have picked up some preconceived ideas of morality that don't fit too well into their mother's divorced life. But it also sounds as if they were extremely distressed by their parents' divorce and are coping with the hurt by effectively blocking out the person they see as responsible. It probably won't help them to be told their father was as responsible for the divorce as you and their mother as that would hurt even more.

If they can't alter their behaviour there are two things you could do. You can put up with the situation but *insist* on politeness from them, if necessary by shaming them in front of someone who matters to them. Or, consoling yourself with the fact that the eldest will virtually have left home once he goes to university, you could encourage the middle child to get his own place to live. Now that he is working he may want to do so anyway, and in the circumstances it would probably be best. It could be made clear that you and his mother will always be there to support him in times of trouble. But he must be told that if, in the meantime, he is so unhappy about you that he is incapable of behaving politely, it is only fair that he should find his own home.

This leaves the thirteen-year-old daughter. Away from her brothers' antagonism, it is very likely that her feelings will change. As she is younger, she may have a more open mind, with fewer preconceived ideas about you. If the worst comes to the worst, at least there would only be one child left in the opposite camp instead of three.

I appreciate you may not want to be seen as the person who is physically displacing the children. Obviously you must gauge just how uncomfortable home circumstances are before making these moves. But you should be entitled to certain consideration in your own home and if your nearly adult stepchildren are unwilling to grant it, they must accept the logical consequences.

PERSONAL ADVICE

Phillip Hodson is a marriage counsellor, local radio 'Agony Uncle' and part-time stepfather to my eldest children (they live with my ex-husband but spend a great deal of time in our home). He sees step-parenthood as having both joys and concerns.

'When you acquire a ready-made family,' he says, 'you acquire young people with values and standards possibly quite different from your own. There may be a culture clash between you, there may be a class difference. Your ideas of children's obedience may not be theirs. Their physical rhythms may differ from yours. If you come from a boisterous family you may not like a shy child and vice versa. You may be jealous of the children or they may be jealous of you. When the chips are down, who will the natural parent choose? You or them? It's uncomfortable to think it might not be you. You have no natural commitment to the child, only indirect acquired commitment. You don't have the natural parent's instinct for doing things for the children without thinking twice and you may not understand what the children expect from you. If stepchildren trade on you – over money, say – you feel resentful. Because there is no natural bond, their needs for money can seem a drain, whereas if it were your own flesh and blood you probably wouldn't think twice about it. No matter what a step-parent may say, it's the spouse you chose to marry, not the children. I think it's vital that the natural parent, and indeed the step-parent too, understands that it is natural *not* to possess the instinctive concern for stepchildren that a real parent has.

'On the other hand, you acquire a ready-made family with none of the hard work involved. You haven't had the exhausting nights, the years of discipline, the childhood diseases to cope with. If you are lucky you may find you now have perfectly charming children who are a pleasure to be with and who adapt easily and readily to their new family life with you. You are wanted and needed by the children as well as by the new partner which, if caring is what you are seeking, may be extremely acceptable. If the children are similar in character to their natural parent whom you love and have chosen to live with, you may find them a double bonus.

'Step-parents won't find that they feel the same about the children year in, year out. They are likely to pass through a number of phases. They may like the kids initially, then find the reality when first living together quite different. Eventually, over the years, you and the kids mellow and improve. One day you realize, with pleasure, that you like them quite a lot.'

How does Phillip suggest a step-parent overcomes the difficulties he outlines?

'Accept reality,' he says, 'don't try to treat the children as if they are your own. Get along with them as well as you can. It will help you to establish house rules and to stick to your promises. Try to cultivate the positive sides of their characters that appeal to you: establish common ground, if you like, over mutual interests and hobbies.

'It's important to realize that they are separate human beings and are entitled to a certain amount of space, just as you are. Don't be a martyr, though. Don't go tearing off to a rock concert you hate, or a film which you know you will loathe just because they want you to. They will learn to take advantage of you that way and ultimately will have no respect for you. But look for films you both want to see, so that you are not continually turning down their approaches.

'I must stress that you have to respect the children as individuals. They should be given their own space and their rights. It's certainly vital to agree with their natural parent *right from the start* what your role is going to be. Are you going to discipline them? There is nothing more undermining than taking a firm line with the children only to find that your spouse is busy refuting your words of wisdom.

'If you can manage to follow this advice, you should be able to feel confident that whatever their eventual reaction is to you, you have done the right thing by them. With any luck, you'll end up enjoying a very happy family life.'

9

Helping Yourself

Becoming a self-help wizard, heavily involved in housing schemes and the provision of day nurseries, may not be your uppermost ambition during the dark days of divorce. But no book on self-help would be complete without a brief mention of what can be inspired by divorce and the needs of working parents.

Nina West was a young Greek woman living in this country who, at the age of nineteen and with a broken marriage behind her, found herself scrubbing floors to support her baby daughter. She never forgot the hardships she endured over housing and care for her child and so, some years later, she founded Nina West Homes. This is a housing association which builds homes for divorced and separated parents and, if there is a local need, sets up nursery schools in the back gardens of the developments. Children under the age of five who live in Nina West Homes can go to these schools and their mothers know that while they are at work their children are being cared for on home ground. The blocks of flats also have a unique intercom system, which enables any parent to plug in from her flat to any other flat in the block. Thus the residents can babysit for one another using this intercom, providing more freedom to go out in the evenings.

Any parent, with support from others, can found a housing association. There are now several major schemes in this country developed around the needs of single parents. What is perhaps not realized is that a housing scheme doesn't just have to build houses. All sorts of other facilities that make life easier and more pleasant can be included. There are schemes which include businesses, communal meeting places, communal laundry facilities – there are even schemes which incorporate a pub!

A housing association enables ordinary members of the public without capital of their own to develop and follow through their ideas, not just of housing but of a lifestyle. A recent development comes from the New Swift Housing Co-operative which, though still in its early stages, plans to provide daycare after school and during the holidays for the children living in these homes.

Any divorcing parent who feels inspired by these tales can seek information on how to set up a housing association from the National Federation of Housing Associations, 30–32 Southampton Street, London WC2.

Back in 1970 a group of women, motivated by their own needs for childcare facilities and a political consciousness about the generally deprived plight of the children of working mothers, managed to set up the Children's Community Centre in North London. It took them over two years to bully the local council into lending them short life property and the funds for conversion. But the Centre eventually opened as a nursery school in 1973 and has managed to carry on ever since. What makes this daycare venture unique is the participation of the parents (both sexes) in the running of the school and care of the children. They have thus managed to keep costs to a minimum, the children receive excellent attention and the parents are still able to work (though restricted to timings made possible by shift work, flexi-time or special arrangements with the employer). The six women who began the scheme were ordinary mothers who felt so strongly that working parents suffer through lack of decent nursery provision that they were determined to set right the injustice, if only on a small scale. If they could do it, so can many others. Information on how the Centre operates and advice on how to set up something similar can be obtained from the Children's Community Centre, 20 Lawford Road, London NW5 (01-267 5300).

WHAT TO DO IF YOU HIT ROCK BOTTOM

Perhaps, however, your needs are more immediate. It is all you can do to last out the day, let alone think about housing schemes. Your grief is such that everything loses its point, there is very little reason for living, you have spent three days in the bath and the aspirin bottle is peculiarly tantalizing.

You can either endure and suffer the days of pain stoically, knowing that even though it is a slow process you will eventually begin to feel better. Or you can go under. If you feel yourself doing that, the best way to keep your sanity is to telephone the Samaritans. The Samaritans provide caring and counselling and you can talk out your problems on the telephone or face to face. They claim over the last twenty-five years to have lowered the suicide rate significantly. The number of your local branch will be in the telephone directory. The number of the head office is 01-626 2277.

EPILOGUE

One of the criticisms of this book will be that I have been viewing divorce through rose-coloured spectacles. How can you reason with a guy wielding a meat axe? Which is precisely why women should develop and use the community, why women in particular should never lose sight of the fact they may need to be breadwinners again, why the unhappy fact of divorce needs to be acknowledged.

I am an optimist. I do believe that, however painful and impossible your divorce seems during its crisis time, your lifestyle will eventually get sorted out and the grief will diminish. When you look back, it is far better for you to know that, however arrangements for the children ultimately turned out, you did your best for them at a time when your own life was at breaking point. We all have strengths and weaknesses. It may be far harder for some of us to cope with distress and grief than it is for others. The best we can do is to provide the happiest background for the children in unhappy circumstances.

Yes, of course the children will be sad their parents no longer live together. But they *need not be permanently damaged* if you and your ex-spouse put them first and remember that they are human beings, not possessions.

Hence my brief inclusion about self-help schemes. Divorce is something that engenders strong feelings. Those strong feelings can be channelled positively into achieving social change, even if only on a small scale. Through building bravely on the experience of marriage break-up we can become happier individuals, and incidentally may help others to be happier too.

Revolutions sometimes start in a small way. Let's hope the divorce revolution recognizes that divorce does *not* signify failure on the part of the participants. Rather, it shows growth and change. People who divorce are people who are reaching out for another state of mind and another stage of their life. What we need to learn is how to change in a *responsible fashion*. Responsibility, I believe, begins with the family.

Divorce and the Law

The legal proceedings of divorce can often make an already thorny relationship even more difficult to cope with. Indeed, some couples who have managed to remain friends during the initial separation find that their solicitor's advice actually creates animosity where previously there had been none.

So it is best to know exactly what your aims are before starting the legal side of marital break-up. This way the solicitor takes instruction from you rather than being your pilot. I am not suggesting you should ignore legal advice but I do think it is important to make sure that you achieve the aims you originally had in mind and don't end up with something quite different.

Having said that, there are of course specific benefits that legal advice can bring, and divorcing couples can derive much benefit from the advice of someone who is not personally involved. A solicitor may, for example, be able to encourage a timid spouse who has been crushed throughout the marriage to be more assertive, or, in the other extreme, to restrain a vindictive spouse from making unfair demands.

CONCILIATION

Conciliation is the term used to describe help given *after* the breakdown of marriage, to enable the parties to deal with the consequences, both emotional and practical. Reconciliation, on the other hand, means an attempt to prevent breakdown occurring or to get the couple back together again.

One of the recommendations of a recent Law Society Report,

entitled *A Better Way Out*, is that counsellors should be able to help people with the tricky emotional experience that the break-up of marriage entails.

Unfortunately, there are not many such counsellors as yet, so self-help is again the best way of dealing with these problems. There is no reason why couples cannot try to help themselves with conciliatory behaviour towards each other.

Conciliation over the children amounts to parents working out for themselves a reasonable system of custody and access that will reflect their children's wishes.

Tom and Cindy's childcare arrangements are a model. They agreed to live near each other (a ten-minute walk) but not too near to be uncomfortable. The children live with Cindy but can visit their father whenever they like.

When, in the early days of divorce, constant meetings were upsetting for both parents, they confined their communication to talking on the telephone. This at least placed some emotional distance between them. They have been living apart for six years now. During that time they have gradually got used to the idea of divorce and are now able to meet and talk to each other quite politely.

The children cycle from one house to the other often. They are able to stay with their father whenever they want to and one or other of them tends to do this about once a fortnight. There's no need to stay more often because they live so close together. Visiting is so relaxed that the two girls feel as much at home with their father as they do with their mother.

It wasn't easy for Tom and Cindy to formulate these arrangements but they kept reminding themselves that it was the children they should think of and not their own hurt feelings. It was a rule which both of them now look back on with relief.

HISTORY OF DIVORCE AND CUSTODY

In the late nineteenth century all parental authority over legitimate children was paternal: the father had rights over any other party, be it mother, State or child. It was not until 1925, when the children's needs were given legal consideration in the Guardianship of Minors Act, that the trend towards awarding care and control to the mother was confirmed by law.

The 1973 Guardianship of Minors Act gave mothers equal rights with fathers over their children and this, coupled with John Bowlby's theories of childcare, which influenced the courts, means that the mother now invariably gets care and control of children under ten, unless there are special circumstances (the most controversial being lesbianism). But changes are being made.

FAMILIES NEED FATHERS

The need for change is highlighted by an organization called Families Need Fathers (see page 72 for their address). Their complaints about custody and access focus on a child's need for *two* parents. A way of achieving this would be for a reasonable representation to be allowed on behalf of the child in the matrimonial court.

The pages of their newsletter are full of personal stories from their members exposing the old-fashioned attitude of judges towards males who are responsible for childcare, towards adultery and towards the 'other people' in a divorce. (On several occasions ex-partners have been refused access until their new lover has left the home. The theory behind this is presumably that the new relationship is an immoral one and will therefore adversely affect the children, and that the impermanence of such a relationship will be harmful.) In the nineteenth century the wife's adulterous conduct automatically deprived her of custody rights and access. Although this is no longer the law, the idea that the person apparently responsible for the marriage breakdown should somehow be punished has unfortunately lingered on.

The Law Society's booklet *A Better Way Out* suggests that there should be only one reason given for divorce, as is the case in Australia. This should be the fact that the marriage has irretrievably broken down, the couple having separated for a period of one year. By removing concepts such as adultery from the statute book they argue that many of these old-fashioned attitudes will be swept away. I wish I could be so certain.

Not all judges are narrow-minded but there is no way of predicting which judge you will get in a child custody dispute, so you need to take these possibilities into account when preparing your case.

THE LEGAL PROCEEDINGS

A divorce is usually conducted in three parts, though there can be separate custody hearings prior to divorce. For further advice, consult a solicitor or a Neighbourhood Law Centre.

There is the actual divorce which, provided both parties consent, can be done through the post. The vast majority (98–99 per cent) go through undefended. If the parties do not consent, each side compiles evidence and a hearing with the judge is arranged.

If there are children, the couple will meet the judge in his chambers to decide on the best arrangements for their welfare. Only if there is a full-scale dispute on care and control and custody will there be a full-scale trial.

If there are mutual property transactions or financial disputes another appointment will be made to discuss maintenance, mutual finance and the settling of capital assets.

CUSTODY AND CARE AND CONTROL

Custody is the right to take long-term decisions which will affect the children's lives, such as which schools they will attend and what religion they should follow. Care and control is the everyday responsibility for looking after them. Usually the judge grants both to one parent. But if the parents agree to opt for joint custody, they share the responsibility for the long-term decisions.

JOINT CUSTODY

The opinion of a member of Families Need Fathers, as expressed in a 1978 Newsletter, is that

> Single custody provides the custodial parent with the ultimate weapon, and settles in a peculiar and perverse manner the power struggles that may have brought the marriage to an end in that it allows the children to be employed as pawns to continue, in a fashion, the marriage in its negative sense. Human nature being what it is, the child ends up a cudgel with which to settle real or imagined grievances. The response of the non-custodial parent is either to disappear forever under the onslaught, or to seek retribution in the form of withholding support payments, engage in child snatching, whatever. Joint or alternating custody would prevent these kinds of incidents.
>
> Joint custody diffuses the potential for unhappy traumatic incidents such as those recently being reported over custody struggles over children originally bound for Australia and elsewhere.
>
> The practice of alternating custody arose not from the courts

themselves but from separating couples who were able to put away their hostilities for the sake of the children. Perhaps the lessening stigma of divorce also lessens mutual guilt and blame.

People trapped in [divorce] conflicts are usually unable to free themselves and at this point the Courts can provide an opportunity to do so by making alternative custody the rule and not the exception. It was argued years ago that duelling was such a natural instinct it could never be outlawed. When it was made illegal, the law was quickly and quietly embraced, freeing many from conflicts that deep down they abhorred but could not back away from.

Joint custody is not a new idea in this country, although it is currently receiving fashionable support. If two parents want joint custody and can convince a judge that they are agreed on their decisions concerning the lives of their family, they are usually awarded it. But if there is a contested application, joint custody is out of the question. The legal brain argues that if two people can't agree *before* the divorce they are not likely to do so after it. For the good of the children, therefore, one parent must be responsible for the decision-making, hence the award of sole custody and care and control. In the long run this will give the children less distress, even if it gives one of the parents more.

I suspect, anyhow, that the FNF author just quoted has slightly missed the point, which is that if the needs of the children are considered to be all-important, custody is not really the burning issue. The everyday care and control is the immediate concern and the $64,000 question is – to which parent should this care and control be given? There is ample evidence to show that (with the exception of very young children) children can live just as happily with Dad as with Mum.

An unfortunate consequence of the psychological pressure put on women by those old theories of 1940s' psychiatrist John Bowlby (even though he did revise them later) is that mothers think they should have care and control of their children even when they *don't really want it*, even if they have never been particularly involved with the children during married life. A Family Court with representation for the children might at least clarify who has been the partner with most childcaring involvement. In Britain, we are a long way off from achieving child representation in law, although one of the projects of the 1979 International Year of the Child was to run a feasibility study on setting up a National Legal Centre. This Centre will specialize in children's cases, and it is proposed that its services will include legal casework, advice, the production of educational material, research, an information service, and test-case work to clarify and develop existing case law about children where legal aid is not available.

But making a parent realize that he or she does not really want custody and care can, in extreme cases, lead to the anguished situation which has cropped up from time to time in America. Imagine the distress of the children when they hear that *neither* parent wants them!

CUSTODY DISPUTE

If there is a custody hearing, both parents may be visited by a court welfare officer when the children are with them. The officer will be a probation officer or a social worker from the local social services department. A welfare report can be instigated by either parent or by the judge. The welfare officer will probably ask the children who they want to live with. The older the children are, the more likely it is that their views will be taken into account.

It is extremely important to make a favourable impression on the welfare officer. His views can be a very persuasive factor in the ultimate judgement.

Points to be considered are:

1   Believe it or not, the cleanliness of your home.
2   The size of the home and the accommodation of the children.
3   The furnishings in the home. For example, custody cases have been lost because there is feminist or radical political literature on view and feminist or radical political posters on the walls. Even nude studies by respected artists are risky, and so are sex magazines.
4   Whether or not your lover is living with you.

While we are on the subject of making impressions, if you do have to appear before a judge, it is sensible to dress 'respectably'. Scruffy jeans are not a good idea.

CUSTODY AND HOUSING

The vexed question is, do you have to have custody to get a house or do you need a house to get custody? The answer appears to be – a bit of both. This isn't the place to go into technical legal disputes but it should be made clear that in a custody dispute you have to show you can provide an adequate home for your kids. Another point is that the final settlement of property in divorce tends to swing to the parent with custody. Judges can order the transfer of council tenancies and privately rented accommodation or that the parent with custody be allowed to remain in the matrimonial home, and they can also transfer the equity of the home (the cash value of the house after the mortgage is deducted) to the parent with custody; this is usually at the cost of reduced or cancelled maintenance payments to the wife, though not to the children.

For detailed help and advice over housing, both the National Council for One Parent Families and Gingerbread can help.

HINTS ON SAFEGUARDING YOUR CASE

The judge's decisions in custody disputes are based on the evidence he hears; on his own personal psychological beliefs about marriage and the family; and on the precedent of divorce cases in recent years. It is vital, therefore, to know what to expect and to take every step to safeguard your interests.

First and foremost, you stand the most chance of keeping your children and being awarded custody if the children are living with you already. So begin the separation period as you mean to go on. Do *not* leave them, however temporarily, with the other partner while you go off to seek another home. *You may not be able to get them back.* And if you do, the children will have been subjected to a tug-of-war fight, however briefly, which is upsetting and damaging. When children are settled into a home it is fairly unusual to see them moved by a court order. A study in 1977 of 855 English and Scottish divorces showed that the children's residences were affected by the court order in less than 1 per cent of cases surveyed. By and large, the children *stayed where they were when the proceedings began.*

Once the children are over the age of six there is a possibility that the custody of boys will be awarded to a father and girls to a mother, on the grounds that children are more likely to need the nurturing of the same sex parent. However, judges tend to dislike splitting up children.

Greater earning power on the part of one parent does *not* automatically mean he or she will be awarded care and control of the children, but the parent must be able to show that he or she can provide a reasonable home for the children. A welfare officer may be called in to provide a professional opinion on the housing conditions and care being proffered. In theory, this sounds reasonable but welfare officers may themselves have fixed theories about the qualities a parent should or should not possess and their word alone can result in a child quite arbitrarily being taken from one parent's home and placed with the other. Automatic children's representation would safeguard against this. As the Law stands now, the children's interest is only represented when the Official Solicitor is called into a case by the judge or on the application of one of the parties, when a particular issue arises.

It helps if you provide evidence that you are a good parent. Keep a diary in which you note down everything that has happened in the past and keep track of what is happening at present. You should include in it your children's statements about who they want to live with and the context in which they were made, their attitude towards your lover, if you have one, and your activities with the children. Everything should be recorded, with dates. If you are in correspondence with your solicitor, include as much of this information as possible in your letters to him.

If you have to get a psychiatrist's report, choose the psychiatrist carefully. The same rule applies to an independent social worker's report. This is where the social workers attached to the National Council for One Parent Families come in useful, because they pride themselves on giving unbiased reports.

If you are living with someone, don't do any swopping about. Stability is all important.

Religion can become a focus of the dispute, as in a case where custody was disputed to a mother who had converted to Judaism and the father objected to the fact that their child (a Christian) might become prey to her Jewish ideas. He ended up with the children. If you can play down anything on these lines which might be controversial, it would be wise.

ACCESS

An access order is an order made by the courts permitting the parent who does not have custody to see the child. It may be a 'reasonable access' order, in which case the parents agree on suitable access arrangements between themselves, or it may be a 'defined' order, where the court sets out definite periods of access in the order, such as each Saturday afternoon from 2 to 6 p.m.

The History of Access
Until 1924 women were not usually granted access to their children,

especially if they had committed adultery. The same rule did not apply to men, however. But since 1962, the courts have stated that either parent has an equal right to access.

Who May Be Granted Access
1 Both the father and the mother of the child.
2 Both the father and the mother of an illegitimate child.
3 A spouse who has treated the child as part of the family although he/she is not the child's natural parent.
4 Grandparents. (Wardship proceedings can be enormously useful for achieving access not easily affected in divorce proceedings; for example, for putting forward extraordinary access proposals, such as access by aunts and uncles.)

How To Get Access
Apply to the court for it.

Qualifications Needed For Access
Access is looked on as a basic right of the parents. It is only denied if the parent is considered to be an 'unfit' person. Access is also officially regarded as a basic right of the children, who should not be deprived of it unless that is in their best interests. The idea of an 'unfit' parent is an ever-changing concept. It's always worth having a try for access.

Reasonable Access
Reasonable access is any arrangement agreed between the parents, without dispute, and approved by the judge. It is up to the parents to work out the arrangements that fit in best with their lifestyle.

Jane and Owen arranged that Jack, aged three, should live with Jane during the week, but should go to his father's house on Friday night and stay there till Monday morning. They also agreed that this arrangement should be flexible because it might not suit Jack when he was older.

Phillipa and David arranged that their two teenage children should visit their father every other weekend and stay with him for at least a week during each of the school holidays. Their father lived some distance away and this was the least disruptive way the children could keep in touch with him and still study for examinations and keep up with their personal friends.

Jenny and Sam lived at opposite ends of the country. They arranged that, while she was little, Zoe should go to school in London and live with her father and stepmother, but during the holidays she should go down to the country to live with her mother and stepfather.

As Zoe grew older, Jenny became more relaxed about motherhood, and wanted to see more of her daughter. Sam felt this was good for Zoe and so the access changed. Zoe then lived most of the time with her mother but spent some of the holidays and most bank holidays with her father. Not all these holidays were in London. On several occasions, Sam and his new wife were very glad to stay with friends in the country near to Jenny.

Isobel and Michael made a point of not seeing each other if possible but overcame their differences for the children's school functions, which they attended together. It was Isobel who cared for the children (they lived with her) but both Michael and his mother played an active part in the children's everyday life. Michael or his mum would often collect them from school, take them off shopping or for tea, and deliver them home at six or seven in the evening. The weekend arrangements were generally that Michael had the children for one day every other weekend, but this too was flexible. He was quite likely to ring Isobel and say, 'I want to take them swimming. How about it?' And, providing it fitted in with everyone's plans, he would do so.

Access Contest

Many of the 'rules' which apply to custody dispute also apply to access contest. It is wise to try and start your access as you mean it to continue. If you can prove to a judge that you have seen your children every other weekend, attended their school functions, taken them to the dentist, taken them regularly to Sunday lunch at their grandmother's, and so on, there is every likelihood that the judge will endorse your behaviour by granting you official permission to continue with it. If, on the other hand, you have been late or not turned up for meetings with the children, or if there has been a period, for whatever reason, when you haven't seen them, this could be fuel for a case against you. This is why it is again wise to keep a written record of your relationship with the children.

Your case for access may be prejudiced by the existence of a lover, and it is not uncommon for access to be granted only when the lover is absent from the home. Certainly it is sensible to stick to one lover only. The welfare officer may visit you for a report too, and the same principles apply to the home background for access claims as they do in a custody dispute.

Disobeying Access Orders

A parent who constantly fails to comply with an access order – for example, by visiting the family at unspecified times and so becoming a nuisance – or a parent with custody who refuses to let the children visit the parent with access runs the risk of going to prison. The chances of this punishment being enforced are slight, however. It happens only in exceptional circumstances where there has been contempt of court, where the parent was in breach of an injunction, or at the very least where an access order was endorsed with a penal notice. What is more likely is that the court will reconsider who should actually have custody.

The parent with custody can claim that the children do not wish to see the parent with access, hence her action in turning away the parent with access. If this is true, she is not in contempt of the court. However, this proviso can be abused because parents with custody can make this claim falsely with little fear of redress.

Another situation which makes the parent with access powerless is when the parent with custody moves away from the district. It can be very difficult keeping up a relationship with your children if you are in Leeds and they are in London. There is no legal way to prevent this, although there are legal ways of contesting the children's removal from the jurisdiction of the English courts, to somewhere like America, for example.

What this all boils down to is that the parent with access is peculiarly vulnerable. Whatever the court order may legally specify, actually getting it put into practice may be quite another matter. You and your children are at the mercy of your ex-spouse. Possession is control.

LESBIAN MOTHERS

Lesbian mothers stand only a small chance of obtaining custody of their children, even if the children are tiny, the mothers are model mothers and the home background is stable and secure. Only a very few women have been awarded custody and those have generally been where either the father or the accommodation he could provide was *so* unsatisfactory that there was no real alternative. The award is usually at the expense of the lesbian relationship, too, since the 'other woman' may be banned from the home or banned from having any physical contact with the mother in front of the children.

Lesbian women who want to bring up their children themselves would be well advised to conceal from the world the fact that they are lesbian. If this is impossible, they should never leave the children with their father other than for access, because they stand a very poor chance of getting them back.

Once they and the children are established in a household, they should do their best to put off and avoid divorce proceedings for *as long as possible, preferably indefinitely.* The longer the children have lived in a settled home with their mother, the more likely they are to be allowed to remain. But, sadly, many children have been removed from settled homes on the premise that anyone else who happens to be heterosexual is preferable as a parent. The children end up with aunts, with housekeepers and with grandmothers, all of whom may be admirable 'parents'. Unfortunately, if the children are very attached to their mother and if they are very young, the emotional hardship is great.

Children of lesbian mothers are likely to be particularly attached to them because there may always have been an element of risk attached to the lesbian household which has heightened the mother's love and caring, and hence the children's too. If there is a suggestion that tomorrow you may never be able to see your mother or child again, you are likely to be intense about that relationship.

So, at present, the best advice seems to be, lie low and hope that your continued good care of the children will count eventually as an important deciding factor with the judge.

HOMOSEXUAL FATHERS

Homosexual fathers are even more unlikely to be awarded custody of their children. I have tracked down only one who has managed it. He appears to have been given custody of his two boys because *everyone* who reported on him to the judge was in favour of his childcaring abilities *including his wife* who stated firmly that she wanted him to care for the children. He has looked after the children for four years now. They have known about his boyfriend for six years (he doesn't live in but visits) and appear to accept this is what's right for their dad. They seem to be healthy little boys who are happy to be living with their father.

GUIDE TO GAY CUSTODY

A booklet, *The Guide to Gay Custody*, is available from Action for Lesbian Parents, 52 Highbury Park, London NW5 2XE. It provides excellent advice and information for gay parents who are fighting custody disputes. Much of the information in it is equally useful for heterosexual couples.

The booklet emphasizes the importance of having a sympathetic and knowledgeable solicitor who is 'on your side'. It also makes the point that you shouldn't be afraid to challenge your solicitor's advice at any stage in the proceedings. If you are completely dissatisfied, it suggests, you should change your solicitor. You are free to do so *at any time.*

REDRESS

All custody hearings can be re-opened at any time during your children's childhood, but I must re-emphasize the importance of starting your divorced life as you mean to go on. Many parents reading this book may want to ignore the advice about keeping a record of their relationship with their children, and keeping an eye on their ex-spouse's activities.

'Ours is a civilized divorce. Why should I want to behave like my husband's enemy?' That's wonderful and hopefully your separation will continue peaceably. But there are many people who have trusted their spouses and who have been appalled to find them behaving exactly as they always swore they wouldn't! If this happens and you haven't kept a record, you might regret it. Because you safeguard your care and control claim to your children does *not* mean you will find yourself in a dispute. It just means you are being careful. Indeed, this is a further opportunity to remind divorcing couples about conciliation. The more you can arrange privately between you, the better chance you have of settling these arrangements well. Those who despair of being able to do this without outside assistance should approach a marriage guidance counsellor or possibly a probation officer for help, and Bristol readers should get in touch with the Bristol Divorce Conciliation service.

LONG-TERM CONCILIATION

Even if a divorced couple do not actually want to see each other or to communicate more than is absolutely necessary, they should still make the effort to keep in touch over the children, even from a distance. After all, the welfare of the children is at stake.

If you need to talk on the telephone, stick to the golden rule of only talking about the children and not about each other. Several couples have found that over the years, those telephone conversations lead to a better relationship and even a type of friendship.

'If we met, he was always nasty to me,' says Adele. 'He'd put me down, make me feel guilty, and then I'd retaliate. That's when we fought over the kids. On the phone he was much calmer, even cracking jokes. Very gradually he began to thaw out on the few times we met.

'It took about five years and his re-marriage, but we have become reasonable friends now. I wish we could be really good friends because I am still very fond of him but that's something he would find impossible. It's a pity. At least we can talk and we nearly always agree over the kids now. The fights were pretty silly really, since we've both got identical feelings about how to raise children.

'I'm glad we were able to avoid each other in those early days and extremely glad we were still able to work out what was best for the children without going to war through our lawyers. This was difficult at the time because I was under pressure both from my lover (who became my second husband) and from my solicitor. But I was convinced I would get better results in the long run if I persevered with Bob on my own.

'It was very tough. He tried to exclude me from their lives by using emotional blackmail, then he argued I was trying to exclude *him*, but we weathered it. I followed my instinct here and I'm very glad I did. By talking to each other over and over again on the phone, and because we helped each other out with the children even though we were both feeling very insecure, we worked out a routine for them and for us. The routine made us all feel better.

'It took guts to keep confronting him – he was very fierce. But it was the right thing to do and we've got happy kids to prove it now. Time *is* a great healer.'

Further Reading

Divorce and After, Gerald Sanctuary and Constance Whitehead (Oyez Publishing 1976)

One Parent Families, edited by Dulan Barber (Teach Yourself Books 1978)

Helping Troubled Children, Michael Rutter (Penguin 1975)

Coping Alone, Elsa Ferri and Hilary Robinson (NFER Publishing 1976)

A Better Way Out – suggestions for the reform of divorce law (The Law Society)

What Every Child Should Like His Parents to Know About Divorce, Dr Lee Salk (Harper and Row 1978)

I want to work . . . but what about the kids? Day care for young children and opportunities for working parents (Equal Opportunities Commission)

Saturday Parent, Peter Rowlands (Unwin Paperbacks, 1981)

Step-parenting, Brenda Maddox (Unwin Paperbacks, 1980)

Surviving the Break-Up, J. S. Wallerstein and J. B. Kelly (Grant McIntyre 1980)

DIVORCE AND YOUR MONEY
W. M. Harper

Money is usually the biggest problem for most married couples about to divorce. What do you do about your house? Can a husband eject his wife from the family home? Can a wife lay claim to her husband's capital or inheritance? Does infidelity affect maintenance? If a wife leaves her husband, will he have to maintain her?

William Harper answers these and many other important questions and sets out advice on a wide range of problems. The author is *not* a lawyer, but has been through the divorce courts in a legal tussle that lasted over seven years. He soon realised that most people caught up in the trauma of divorce don't understand how the courts work or how the divorce will affect them financially. This book is written to help others avoid the difficulties he encountered through ignorance of the law.

'sets out in a relaxed and readable way to show all husbands and wives what their respective financial rights and obligations will be'

Good Housekeeping

'answers the questions ordinary people are likely to ask when entering the divorce stakes'

Financial Weekly

AN A–Z OF CHILDREN'S EMOTIONAL PROBLEMS
Tom Crabtree

All children go through problem patches: times when they're difficult to understand, moody and miserable or when they're faced with situations with which they cannot cope. This book provides parents with exactly the practical, down-to-earth advice they need to help them through the times of emotional crisis with their children that are part-and-parcel of modern family life. This is not a book of psychiatric theorizing, but aims to do three things: to reassure parents that, whatever their child's problem, they are not alone; to give advice on what to *do* with the child and, finally, to tell them what help is available if the problem becomes too serious for the parents to cope with alone.

There are over a hundred entries arranged alphabetically, and, from shyness to exam phobia, stealing to thumb sucking, Tom Crabtree offers sensible, balanced advice for worried adults treading the tricky path of parenthood.

STEP-PARENTING
How to Live with Other People's Children
Brenda Maddox

An epidemic of divorce is sweeping through all the countries of the world that observe Western marriage customs. Many more people are attempting the difficult task of replacing a parent. But for every happy step-relationship there are dozens dogged by bewilderment, resentment, guilt and even downright dislike, often not of the step-parent's making.

What are your rights and duties? How can you reassure the troubled children of a broken marriage, or win the affection of a hostile child? Brenda Maddox deals with these and many other questions. She also discusses the myths and facts of the subject and vividly describes her own experience as a step-parent.

'Covers the whole gamut of step-problems in an entertaining and informative way'

Sunday Times

'The general effect of her compassionate and interesting book is helpful and comforting'

She

SATURDAY PARENT
Peter Rowlands

This book is for the 'Saturday Parent' who lives apart from his or her children and sees them only at weekends, or for holidays, or every so often. Peter Rowlands, himself a Saturday parent and also the author of several books about children, discusses the many questions that arise in these circumstances.

In order to write *Saturday Parent*, he interviewed many Saturday parents and their children. Their histories clearly show how important – and how worthwhile – it is to stay in touch with your children even though you no longer live together. For divorced or separated parents this book should be essential reading. It will also be valuable for anyone whose job it is to look after children, such as teachers or social workers, and for grandparents and others closely involved with families that have split up.

'Peter Rowlands's ideas on dealing with the problems and pitfalls that may arise are both imaginative and practical'

Times Educational Supplement

'Much constructive advice . . . Peter Rowlands emphasises the importance of keeping communication with the child at a very personal and flexible level'

Nursery World